Liberal Education
and
Careers Today

by Howard Figler

Director, Career Center
University of Texas at Austin

About the author...

Howard Figler has been Director of the Career Center at the University of Texas since 1982. From 1970 to 1982, he was Director of the Counseling and Career Center at Dickinson College in Carlisle, PA.

Dr. Figler's areas of interest include the dynamics of the job search process, psychological concerns in career counseling, and the roles that values play in career decision making. His publications include **The Complete Job Search Handbook** (Henry Holt, 1988); **PATH: A Career Workbook for Liberal Arts Students,** 2nd Edition (Carroll Press, 1979); **The Athlete's Game Plan for College and Career** with Stephen K. Figler (Peterson's Guides, 1984); and **Outreach in Counseling** with David J. Drum (Intext, 1973).

The author's appreciation for liberal education began with his Bachelor of Arts program at Emory University (1960). He then completed a Master of Business Administration Degree at New York University (1961), and a PhD in Educational Research and Testing at Florida State University (1968).

```
            Library of Congress Cataloging-in-Publication Data


Figler, Howard E.
     Liberal education and careers today / by Howard Figler.
        p.   cm.
     Bibliography: p.
     Includes index.
     ISBN 0-912048-64-6 : $10.95
     1. Vocational guidance--United States.  2. College graduates-
  -Employment--United States.  3. Bachelor of arts degree.  4. Master
  of arts degree.   I. Title.
  HF5382.65.F53  1989
  650.1'4--dc19                                             88-33362
                                                            CIP
```

Published and distributed by
the Garrett Park Press
P.O. Box 190B
Garrett Park, MD 20896

Table of Contents

Acknowledgements

Acknowledgements

This book became a reality when Bob Calvert, publisher of the Garrett Park Press, transformed my ideas, notes, references, and deep convications about liberal arts into a book format. His own fine book **Career Patterns of Liberal Arts Graduates** (Carroll Press, 1969) summarizes one of the first major research studies on the outcomes of liberal education.

The many supportive articles and publications about the careers of liberal arts graduates, as noted in this book, reinforce my feeling that the marketplace has abundant respect for liberal education. The many authors whose writings provide better understanding of the power of liberal education provide the real background for this book.

A special debt is owed to the liberal arts graduates who are featured in the career profiles and who provided the material and the consent for their citations.

My years of counseling liberal arts students at Dickinson College and the University of Texas and work with individual faculty members concerned with developing a broad based education for life provided a reservoir of motivation which overflowed into this book. I remain forever biased that the broad and deep approach to learning uplifts the person and permits him or her to approach career and other problems with the confidence that an able mind and open spirit can deal with anything.

Howard Figler

Austin, Texas
December 1988

Section 1
Why This Book?

In my first year as a liberal arts career planning director I began to hear people make comments such as:

"A liberal Arts degree is worthless in the job market."
"All you can do with it is teach, go to graduate school, or hope for a wealthy spouse."

"Maybe a liberal education was OK generations ago but today's technological society requires specialization in college."

Since I was a career counselor working with liberal arts students, these opinions made me decidedly uncomfortable. And I did not enjoy seeing the contortions my students went through to make themselves "marketable":

- They looked for the most "practical courses," too often neglecting others which they perceived as "not relevant to my future career."
- They took double majors and other curricular combinations in the hope that they would come up with the magic formula for career success.
- They bucked hard to get into specialized master's level programs on the assumption that they could not do anything with a mere liberal arts bachelor's degree.

Such strategies seemed both illusory and unnecessary to me. Far too many students and their parents assumed that a college transcript and its courses had to be sold as so many chunks of knowledge with direct vocational implications. By contrast, I sensed that a liberal education prepared a person for employment in a way that transcended the titles of courses. Yet it was difficult to explain this to students, or their families, and to persuade them that liberal learning by itself had merit. There was widespread fear among liberal arts students that they were destined to become second-class citizens in the job market. They yearned for someone with satisfactory answers to the question, "What can I do with my liberal arts major?"

And when I turned for help to my potential allies, liberal arts faculty members, too often their reactions were defensive ("no need to worry about careers"), resistant ("it's not my job"), or no reaction at all ("let's talk about it some other time"). This lowered my own morale a notch and frustrated students. Many expressed their displeasure or concern to their friends and siblings who followed them and liberal arts admissions offices began to feel the pressure of "vocationalism" among students. Before long, fully one-fourth of all undergraduate students were in business majors. And, in response, many liberal arts colleges began to offer a more vocational curriculum to compete for the new career-minded students.

"The well prepared manager of the next generation will simply need more than that nation's graduate schools of business can provide. Those needs can be best addressed in the liberal arts...Managers in the next generation must understand foreign cultures, languages, politics, and business practices."

Professor G. C. Parker,
Stanford Business School

1

It was a difficult time for the advocates of traditional liberal education. The word got around that liberal arts might be in trouble. I didn't know what would happen but hoped that the academic and employer communities might provide some reassurance about the merits of liberal education in the market place. I began an intensive study of professional journals, popular media, and research studies to look for appropriate evidence.

I searched for reports, opinions, anything I could find which would help illuminate the status of liberal arts graduates in today's employment world. Admittedly, I began with a double bias believing, first, that liberal education is the richest, most enduring form of learning and is urgently needed in the collegiate programs of tomorrow's leaders for both business organizations and governmental community service groups. Second, I could not imagine that liberal arts graduates fell into a well soon after graduation and were never heard from again.

I did not want liberal arts graduates to lower their aspirations because of misperceptions about their desirability as employees. It bothered me to see students forcing themselves to take subjects of little or no interest to them. Too many students were studying debts, credits, and balance sheets when they could be learning basic principles of problem solving (science), logic (philosophy), research (history) and analysis of human motivation (English literature). I felt that learning how to think would be far more valuable on the job than learning the nuts and bolts of specific occupations, when they would be restrained on the job anyway. It seemed ludicrous that students (and their parents too) made such a big deal over pre-vocational courses that offer only a marginal advantage at entry-level, an advantage that is quite obliterated after six months on the job.

The responses from the academic and employment communities started slowly but they gathered steam in recent years and the result has been the assembling of a broad base of information on the merits of liberal education in a career; an extensive file of studies, books, and reports on liberal education and careers; and a body of useful suggestions which may help those studying liberal arts today or those working with them as faculty members, career advisers, or placement counselors.

The net result was like awakening a sleeping giant. Judging from the number of useful reports and comments on this theme, and the consistency of their support for a liberal arts degree, the bells are tolling today not for its funeral but are ringing in praise of its value.

The goal of this book is to help liberal arts graduates realize they can walk into job interviews like lions, not lambs. They should be respected as the leaders of tomorrow, not looked upon by skeptics as neophytes who lack direction and, therefore, ended up in liberal arts studies. Liberal arts graduates can live up to their traditional reputation instead of having to live down recent mythology which depicted them as misguided intellectuals.

2

Section 2

How This Book Can Help You

"The most important issues have subjective and qualitative dimensions, which are best approached through history, literature, art, and social sciences...This is as true for leadership in engineering as it is for leadership in public policy."

Dean James Gibbons,
College of Engineering,
Stanford University

I hope you don't regard this as a book about how to get a job. Most of what follows describes how and why liberal arts graduates are suitable candidates for a wide range of positions today. This book will also help you organize your strategy for obtaining employment. Nevertheless, if you view this book as a job hunting manual, you have missed the point.

College graduates, liberal arts alumni included, are going to be hired with or without this book. Why? Because, unless you wandered into higher education by accident and somehow stumbled through to a degree by doing the absolute minimum, you are a college graduate who has these qualities: (1) you are well-educated, (2) you have high achievement motivation, and (3) you have developed a lot of skills that are attractive to employers. You can work with people, you read quickly and with depth, you know how to analyze and solve problems, and you are ambitious enough to want to do a job well.

These are the very things that employers prize the most. They are going to help you get hired in a lot of places, especially when you compete with people who are less well-educated, who lack basic learning skills, who do not communicate as well as you, who are often less motivated, and who are poor candidates for additional training.

Successful job hunting for the college graduate is not just getting someone to hire you for any job. Here are some goals worthy of your education:

(1) Don't settle for job security.

Go for a situation that takes real advantage of your talents, not just one that happens to be readily available. This means you must enter the land of risk, look at different options, perhaps wait a bit longer, and suffer some anxiety. Trust me, and others who have gone before you. It's worth the trouble.

(2) Don't take a job that undernourishes your spirit.

Don't waste your employment potential just to get hired as a salesperson of candy pebble machines to supermarkets. Look for a job where you feel the work is important, and makes a difference to someone, The kind of job, when asked what you do, you can talk about with pride. If making money is important to you, get involved with a product or service that you value, one that you will want to identify with. Long after you have established yourself in the job market, it is your spiritual bank account that will matter most.

(3) Don't take a job for status alone.

Signing with a household name corporation or entering a "respectable" profession may be nice to talk about to your friends and family but it doesn't last if you chose that career

3

largely for reasons of identity. In the rush to get settled in the world of work, or to give your parents the answer to the question "What is little Freebush doing?", you may enter a line of work mostly because it is handy and sounds good. Look a little closer. Does the job fit who you are as a person? Are you challenged, maybe even inspired, by what goes on there, or is it just a place to hang your hat?

(4) Don't take a job that compromises your personal values.

You can only shut your eyes to questionable practices so long before you get eyestrain and headaches and wish you were somewhere else. Take a good look at how prospective employers deal with people, both those they employ and those they serve as customers or clients. Will you be pleased to tell others about your work or will you end up having to defend practices you're not sure you agree with?

(5) Do take a job where there is challenge and an opportunity for future leadership.

Any job, no matter how secure or interesting on the surface, will mean little if you are stuck a few years later just maintaining yourself, running in place. You will want an opportunity to direct, lead, have a say in future polity of the work you are doing. Take a job where this potential is visible, even if there is no guarantee. Talk with present leaders about the problems and future directions of the organization. Can you see yourself moving into chairs of greater responsibility? If that picture looks cloudy, or downright bleak, move along and look at something else.

Measure your job opportunities on the five scales cited above, The more each job has of these, the better it fits your index of Good Work. Use the ideas in this book to help you locate jobs that push up your spiritual index. Don't get stuck thinking that survival is what the work world is about. Reach high and let your abilities and sensibilities come into play. Find yourself some Good Work, develop it, and make it your own. Anything else is less than you deserve.

Liberal arts, I believe, is superior preparation for Good Work, because it encourages you to think first about values, challenge, opportunity, leadership, and spiritual nourishment — rather than status and job security.

"Students trained in the liberal arts are better able to formulate valid concepts, analyze arguments, define themselves, and orient themselves maturely to the world. The liberal education...also seems to increase the leadership motivation patterns - a desire for power, tempered by self control."

A New Case for Liberal Arts

4

Section 3

Ten Reasons Why Employers May Not
Hire a Liberal Arts Graduate
(But Later On They Will Wish They Had)

"There is a place—and a central place—or the humanities and liberal arts graduates in business; that's good news. The bad news is that the good news is not better known."

Charles L. Brown
Chairman, AT&T

"I believe that businesses should go back to basics in recruiting, should forget about business schools and recruit the best liberal arts students we can find...What is desperately needed in an increasingly complex world dominated by technicians is the skepticism and sense of history that a liberal arts education provides. History, philosophy, logic, English literature are more important to deal with today's problems than great technical competence."

Felix Rohatyn
From Commencement Address at Long Island University
(New York Times, June 3, 1987)

Employers are going to be an important part of your future world. If you are to work sucessfully with them, and to elicit a suitable offer of employment, it helps to understand their point-of-view. Listed below are 10 indictments for which liberal arts graduates may be "guilty" as charged. They offer certain qualities to employers and demonstrate other behaviors that may be unsettling. Consequently, employers may resist hiring liberal arts graduates for these reasons. Your job is to recognize them as some of the virtues of a liberal arts education, rather than being defensive about them. Be patient and look for situations where these attributes will be appreciated.

(1) Liberal Arts Graduates get bored easily.

If you don't keep them occupied with something new to learn they get restless and sometimes ornery at work. They bug the other workers for things to do and look around for new problems to be solved. This same restlessness may lead liberal arts graduates to change jobs (either within the organization or leaving for a different employer) once they feel they have fulfilled their usefulness.

(2) They don't fit into any department.

It is sometimes difficult for an organization to figure out where liberal arts graduates "belong" because their fields of study do not mesh neatly with any particular corporate department. Hence, the organization has to work a little harder to decide where the graduate can make the best contribution. Meanwhile, liberal arts graduates are twiddling their thumbs, recognizing that they could be used in any of several departments, hoping that their versatility will be recognized and used to advantage.

(3) Liberal Arts Graduates Get Other Workers Irritated At Them.

They do nasty things like spotting grammatical errors or spelling errors in memos or letters and calling attention to them before they are sent out....or they may speak with the visitor from France or Mexico in the language they learned during college....or they may understand what the boss means when she says: "We have just scored a Pyrrhic victory," staying silent while everyone else applauds. In other words, those extra dimensions of learning which characterize a broad education can stir temporary resentment, particularly if the liberal arts graduate flaunts them. However, if he or she has cultivated some communication skills along the way, these little extras can be turned into assets.

(4) Liberal Arts Graduates Will Be Pests.

Like little children who still have the curiosity with which they were born, liberal arts graduates want to know "why" everything is done in a particular way. They will question company routines, habitual ways of solving problems or responding to customer requests, and the usual explanations for "the way things are done around here." Liberal arts encourages investigative and reflective attitudes. These may upset people at first because it makes them think a little harder about their established procedures. Eventually, the liberal arts graduate's "pest quality" may lead to improved methods, solved problems, and greater productivity.

(5) Liberal Arts Graduates Will Be Reading On The Job.

Heaven only knows what they'll be reading, even when they are supposed to be "working." Perhaps a best-selling management book related to the way the department is organized or **The Wall Street Journal** to see what the competition may be doing. Or maybe a psychology textbook about co-dependency to learn how employees or family members may unwittingly contribute to a co-worker's alcoholism or an issue of **American Demographics** to note population trends which may affect the types of products needed ten years from now. All this when they are supposed to be concentrating on the tasks at hand. What's a supervisor to do about this? If such reading is not evidence of boredom, but the liberal arts graduate's desire to get to the bottom of an office concern, then a supervisor may even learn to welcome this kind of behavior. If not, the graduate will probably seek a different avenue, where such "outside reading" is encouraged.

(6) Liberal Arts Graduates Will Want to Attend the Concert This Evening with Their Spouses or Friends, Instead of Working Late at the Office.

The liberal arts graduate will allow family life to intrude upon total dedication to the job, clearly a sign of subversion if there ever was one. Not only that, they'll probably want to talk about the concert the next day at the office. This kind of behavior is revealed by other workers as well, not just liberal arts alumni, but it seems especially characteristic of the graduate who values a balance and integration between his or her personal and work lives. Working late and long is a religion peculiar to American industry but the liberal arts graduate persists in finding ways to do an effective and productive job, while still making time for family life and outside pursuits. It takes a little extra creativity and ingenuity to juggle these various priorities, but the liberal arts graduate and others who balance work and family like it that way, and

6

when they occasionally see the boss with theatre tickets in his or her pocket, they don't feel so bad after all.

(7) Liberal Art Graduates Will Want to go Back to School.

Just when you get 'em trained properly, they'll be talking about an MBA degree, a law degree, a program in public administration, or some other program of study that will take them away from the job. Is there no loyalty? Can't they overcome the urges to study and learn? Are they really not interested in working? Liberal arts graduates will look around for new learning, but they often will do it to enhance their skills in their present jobs, or perhaps to aspire to higher levels in the organization. They do have a greater inclination toward advanced study than other college grads, but this is not necessarily a problem for the employer. It can be an asset. Willingness to study is willingness to grow, and acquire new skills and knowledge that a company needs (language skills, technical knowledge, financial skills, etc.). Many alert liberal arts graduates will see the needs of the employer, recognize these as avenues of career promise, and will enroll in graduate programs that enable them to help the employer after they have completed their studies.

(8) Liberal Arts Graduates Will Want to Work in Other Countries.

First thing you know, the graduate will be applying for an appointment in France or Brazil, to see the places they studied about in school and which often leads to exciting side trips on the weekends. How will the employer keep them on the company farm, after they've seen Paree? Yes, the liberal arts graduate has a greater-than-average impulse toward working and living outside the U.S. but this can be translated into an advantage for the employer. Language skills, an inclination toward learning other cultures, and a willingness to take the risks of foreign living are all virtues. The company which wants to establish foreign markets can use liberal arts graduates toward this end. People who handle themselves well in other countries are in short supply, yet organizations need them if they are to succeed in foreign ventures. The overseas assignment will not be as exotic and romantic as the typical graduate may believe, but he or she will typically have a desire to give it a try and the learning background to integrate well in the new situation.

(9) Liberal Arts Graduates will be Subversive.

They will continually do things that disturb the status quo and are critical of the organization's operations. Liberal arts graduates will complain that the company's product is not good enough, that the store is overlooking key customer needs, and perhaps that the company is losing favor in the community because of some of its policies. They will nag and

"The term 'liberal arts' is derived from the Latin artes liber ales, the higher arts, which in early Roman times were accessible only to freshmen (liberi). But the tradition of liberal education dates back at least to Greece, to Plato and his Academy with its devotion to truth and learning for their own sakes."

Career Patterns of Liberal Arts Graduates

7

needle, and take side with the public, often to the irritation of managers and leaders of the organization. Sometimes this will even get them fired, because they have not learned the delicate art of timing and diplomacy, or because they have not learned how to acquire support for their ideas. But, sometimes too the graduate's complaints will bring to light a key problem, and lead to improved service or change of product. Maybe it was a liberal arts graduate who first urged the child-proof drug container, or who stimulated the invention of Velcro for backpackers tired of fumbling with complicated straps. In any work situation, you can expect liberal arts graduates to view the company's products with a careful eye and speak up when they think something ought to be different. Complaining is a form of dedication.

(10) Liberal Arts Graduates will have Wild Ideas.

Perhaps the best reason to view liberal arts graduates with some skepticism is that they have big ideas, some of which simply do not fly. They'll propose new services that won't work, they'll challenge prevailing viewpoints, and they'll even say crazy things like: "Alexander the Great was a model CEO. Look at how he ran that empire based on principles of modern management." Liberal arts graduates just wanna have fun. And they want to do it by looking at old problems in new ways. Or new problems in old ways. They do not have a "business as usual" attitude. They look for ways to innovate, on the premise that the needs of any customers, clientele, or constituency are continually changing. Taxpayers want different services than they used to have. Home owners want different products. Office managers need equipment to keep productivity in pace with technological advances. Skateboarders need new designs to dream up new tricks. And so it goes.

Employers can find a lot of reasons to resist liberal arts graduates, but many of these would be shortsighted, because the creativity and persnickity-ness of the graduates often yields large dividends. Liberal arts graduates can shake up established office routines, but they usually do it because they are looking for a better mousetrap, or trying to make a better connection between an organization and the people it is trying to serve. Hiring the liberal arts graduate is a prescription for change that is generally productive and growth-producing.

"A teacher affects eternity; he can never tell where his influence stops."

Historian Henry Adams

CAREER PROFILE

*"I get joked all the time about my coming here and saying,
'I can do anything. Any job you have, I can do it.'"*

Susan House
BA English 1976
Now, Vice President, Media Director
Yudell Communications

Liberal Arts Education
I feel like the variety of things I learned in liberal arts has helped me to deal with anything that might come up, rather than limiting me to one specific area. It's helped me to know and understand a broad range of activities and people.

I was an English major and I also took about 24 credits in fine arts. I find I really use my English background. Everyone in the agency comes to me with grammar questions, and everything that leaves the agency has to pass in front of me for review before it goes to press.

Job Search Techniques/Results
The idea of a job in advertising appealed to me, because it seemed like it would be interesting and exciting. It wouldn't be a boring, routine job, and it would allow me to use my English skills.

When I first got out of school, I worked four different jobs for a temporary service and at each new place I talked about wanting to get into advertising in some capacity. There weren't any permanent job openings at any of these places, but the last place I worked referred me here (Yudell Communications). They needed someone to do an interim assignment. So I came out here, where I worked coordinating advertising materials like tearsheets, reprints, printed samples, etc., into the portfolio books for each client.

That assignment lasted about two months, and because they already had their positions filled, I went to work for Dunn and Bradstreet as a business analyst. There I analyzed businesses in the Houston area. Shortly after that, Yudell Communications called me back and offered me the job of Media Director. I knew the company and knew that I wanted to work there, so I accepted the offer.

At that point my job was buying media—all types of media—newspaper, magazines, radio, television, outdoor, everything. I also prepared budgets for all of our accounts, allocating how much would go to each media area. I'm still doing that, and am also managing the office, supervising the bookkeeping department, doing general account services, and handling interviewing and hiring for the company.

Job Advice
In this business, it's important that you have a degree, but the kind of degree is not so important. Don't worry about whether or not your degree exactly matches the description of the job that interests you. You learn about your job by being a part of things. For instance, I've learned everything I know about business here—not in school. Either you learn or you're gone.

Liberal arts students that want to get into advertising should start out accepting any available position, regardless of whether or not they think it's beneath them. Once you've got your foot in the door, it's pretty easy to progress. Also, knock on doors. Every May and December we get tons of resumes, but they never follow up on them. We usually end up throwing them away.

If somebody came to our office it would be a very different story. My employer has hired two or three people that have just come to the door and said, "Here I am."

Have confidence. I get joked all the time about my coming here and saying, "I can do anything. Any job you have, I can do it." Even if it comes across as being a little too much, employers tend to look upon a confident applicant favorably.

Section 4

More on the Value of Liberal Arts In The Workplace

"If I could choose one degree for the people I hire it would be English...You can teach a pack of Cub Scouts how to do portfolio analysis."

Senior Vice-President,
First Atlanta Corporation

The liberal arts graduate is hireable and promotable in almost every sector of the world of work. Executives and managers attest to this, research studies confirm it, and the general public is becoming increasing aware as well. Nevertheless, too many of today's liberal arts students are skeptical about their job prospects.

These students see the job sheets posted outside college placement offices and note frequent employer listings for engineering, accounting, computer science graduates. Yet, many of these same companies have dozens of liberal arts alumni in top management and staff positions. What's the answer?

Three statements can be made that transcend any argument about the relative merits of liberal education versus other training:

(1) What employers want most from college graduates are clear and imaginative thinking, diverse communication skills, and the ability to work well with a variety of people.

(2) These qualities are needed by all college graduates who intend to advance in their careers, not just liberal arts graduates. Those who lead academic programs can ask themselves: " Are we producing qualities in our graduates that will enable them to take on responsibility and solve problems that we cannot even foresee? Or, are we just training knowledgeable people who will become good technicians, bridgebuilders, and analysts who lack the capacity to lead or address broader concerns?"

(3) Liberal arts graduates do not obtain these important skills from particular courses or from major fields of study, but from an entire curriculum and its teachers, which emphasize inquiry, dialogue, coherent expression, universal problems, critique, and cross-disciplinary thinking. It must have been a liberal arts graduate who said, when the railroads began their decline: "We're not in the railroad business, we're in the transportation business".

"We frequently see straight A students who can't make the cut. A pathetic preoccupation with marks seems to clog the entryway for other experiences.
Communications skills — both written and oral — are extremely important. Can the candidates express their ideas and thoughts convincingly, clearly?

Dr. Robert K. Armstrong,
Manager, College Relations
E.I. Dupont de Nemours

For example, it takes more than a chemistry major to address the pollution concerns of a corporation. Company leaders must examine the politics of the community, the economics of waste disposal, the sociology of land use planning, employee relations, ethical concerns, language problems with leaders must examine the politics of the community, the economics of waste disposal, the sociology of land use planning, employee relations, ethical concerns, language problems with local residents, and the mathematics of water flow if discharge methods are changes.

Most any college-level job draws on knowledge from many disciplines. Let's take an everyday example. Suppose you're an up-and-coming manager in a graphics design firm. You have to know or learn about art, economics, the psychology of consumer behavior, the sociology of union workers, the philosophy of your client's publications, and the mathematics of arranging copy and art to fit a printed page. Or lobbying, a job that would seem to "fit" students of government, draws also on the sociology of voter patterns, understanding other cultures (ethnic voters), the psychology of persuasion, and the mathematics of budgetary allocations.

"The major problems encountered in the business world deal with human nature, human error, and human understanding."

St. Louis University graduate

Liberal, Not Vocational, Skills

By emphasizing relationships between formal education and work, teachers have unwittingly cultivated the idea that job attainment is related to what you know. In fact, the reverse theme is closer to the truth. Those who make a difference in their work are continually engaged with what they don't know. To illustrate:

(1) **Decisions on Partial Information:** Picture the marketing executive who must decide how to distribute and promote a new product, or anyone who must reckon with alternative futures. He/She must commit millions in the face of what he/she knows little about.

(2) **Interpreting Foreign Tongues:** Imagine the administrator who must deal with computer languages, government jargon, scholarly terms, mathematical notation, or artist's representations of a foreign culture; he/she must grasp the essentials of a new technology or art form by interpreting what the natives are saying and, in the next breath, translating these new ideas into action.

(3) **Mediating Between Interest Groups:** So many decisions which affect people's lives are made by others who know little of their predicament. Consider the government leader who funds projects he/she will never see, the college president who negotiates between trustees and faculty, but lives in the world of neither, and the corporate manager who mediates between a stockholding public he/she seldom hears and all-but-invisible clientele.

(4) **Dealing with the Unknowable:** Highest levels of responsibility are reserved for those who grapple directly with

"Knowledge is capable of being its own end. Such is the constitution of the human mind that any kind of knowledge, if it be really such, is its own reward."

John Cardinal Newman, <u>The Idea of a University</u>

The six skills required for today's world of work are reading, writing, speaking and listening, mathematics, reasoning, and studying.

The College Board, <u>Academic Preparation and College</u>

It is their talent for handling the unknowable and even creating new ideas and constructs from it, which set the leaders apart from technicians.

The ability to deal effectively with what one doesn't know derives from what I shall call the "liberal skills." These skills relate not to specific tasks, motions, or operations, but to those capacities which can be generalized beyond themselves to a wide variety of contexts.

Liberal Skills

For the student who doesn't engage in a vocational major, who lacks "practical" education, it is often said that he/she needs some sort of "skills" to qualify for good employment. We must be careful of this word "skills." I am uncomfortable with the ways in which it is usually interpreted. It calls forth images of some bygone era, when a person had to learn a manual trade or be familiar with a certain product in order to gain employment.

As Peter Drucker, the noted management consultant tells us, we live now in the era of "knowledge jobs," jobs which depend upon information and concepts, rather than upon products or the manufacturing process. Teaching, management, consultation, administration, and many others are all "knowledge jobs." There are two things to note about such jobs: (1) The skills necessary for knowledge jobs can be transferred from one company to another, one industry to another; (2) Many of these skills are not only taught in a classroom or theoretical context, but also are available through total life experiences.

I am speaking, of course, of the wide range of "universal" skills that are so important to personal attainment, so crucial to corporate growth, and so absolutely vital to personal satisfaction, that we simply forget they even exist.

Despite some employers' insistence upon "marketable skills" from new college graduates, we must look carefully at what they mean by "skills."

> Thus the skills employers are looking for in graduates are not specific to a machine or industry; they want young workers who can read, write, compute, pick up new skills quickly and eagerly, and interact cooperatively with others. These are the adaptive skills of liberal education, not the specific skills of vocational education. (O'Toole, <u>Change</u>, 1975)

Thus, when a college student asks you: "What can I do during college that will improve my chances of advancing in the world of work?", don't waste his/her time talking about course selections, how to study harder, or doors that will be opened by the college degree. Instead, speak to him/her on the "liberal skills."

13

Communication Skills: Writing reports, essays, and correspondence in plain language; speaking effectively to individuals and to groups; listening carefully and empathetically whenever necessary; portraying ideas clearly and imaginatively in visual media, etc.

Thinking Skills: Defining a problem cogently; evaluating alternative courses of action critically; creating divergent solutions to a problem when more than one answer is possible; shaping new ideas in the context of old circumstances.

Human Relations Skills: Interacting cooperatively with superiors, subordinates and peers; communicating orders, instructions, and feelings with openness, genuineness, and understanding. Delegating tasks in ways which show respect for the other person and receptivity to his/her ideas.

Valuing Skills: The ability to view and assess an area of work activity in terms of the effects it will have upon human welfare, and the ability to make and enforce decisions in terms that will maximize such welfare.

Detective Skills: Discovering and identifying people who have information that is relevant to a task or problem, and identifying resource materials which are necessary for solution of the problem.

Interviewing Skills: Acquiring information from people, when the people may be difficult to reach, or reluctant to divulge information. Generating trust in such situations, necessary for future contacts.

Self-Marketing Skills: The ability to sense an idea whose time has come, move toward work modes that capitalize upon this idea, and sell this idea to appropriate people.

Though I refer to these as liberal skills, it does not follow that these necessarily derive from the liberal education. Such skills can be nourished anywhere, in vocational programs, non-educational experiences, or any other context where the individual can refine his/her personal attributes. The students who decide that liberal skills are important to them will not allow a curricular bias to stand in their way.

Even a liberal subject taught in a liberal way does not ensure the emergence of liberal skills. The teacher and the college can provide the environment where a student may grapple with uncertainty, but the student may reject these opportunities if he/she chooses. There are always paths of least resistance available, if one looks hard enough.

Career Profiles: Alumni Comments

All of the following men and women are liberal arts graduates of Dickinson College in Pennsylvania. Each responded to my request for their evaluation of the value of liberal education in their careers.

The diversity of their careers reflects the options open to those with a good general education. Their lives and careers, like all of us, are full of pluses and minuses, ups and downs. These letters were written at a fairly early stage in their careers and advancements and promotions will come later. It is important for readers to sense that new graduates have to struggle in almost any field but that each survives in his or her own way and gains maturity from it.

After each is a Counselor's Summary made shortly after the letter was received. Actually, quite a few years ago.

PATRICIA TORRES
Historic Preservationist
Major-Art History

"When I think of the period immediately before and after graduation I still get an uneasy feeling in my stomach. Let's face it; the job market is less than fantastic. As an art history major I wasn't headed to graduate school and the Museum Of Modern Art was not clamoring at my door with a job offer. Unhappily, I headed to Colorado where my parents live—and where room and board were free. Would "real life" ever begin?

There were no jobs in Denver in an art-related field. While waitressing for a few months to earn some money, I decided that my interests were more within the field of historic preservation.

I decided that since I couldn't get a "real" job, I would do volunteer work in a field that I considered extremely interesting and might lead to a job. During the fall I divided my time between working in the Congressman's district and campaign offices and wrote articles for the monthly newspaper published by "Historic Denver"—the largest private preservation group in the country.

Both volunteer jobs ultimately paid off; I was offered a job in my Congressman's office in Washington which enabled me to get some solid work experience back East where I wanted to live. While there I continued to write articles for Historic Denver's newspaper and was in a position to meet people in preservation-related fields.

That all happened three years ago. Since that time I have pursued graduate school (I'm now going through the painful process of writing my thesis) and have a job in the historic preservation field (US Dept. of Interior). It's time to figure out my next course of action. At this point I have the wild idea that I'll quit about this time next year and live in Italy for a year. Hopefully, I'll be accepted to an architectural conservation course at the U. of Rome. Even if I'm not, I'll try to work something out.

I'm not sure where I want to live or exactly what phase of preservation work I want to pursue. Crazy as this may sound I think I'm experiencing a sort of mid-20's crisis. I hate to see what I'll be like at 40!

Graduates of liberal arts colleges, worried by what they perceive as a lack of "marketability" on their part, too often hasten to get that MBA or law degree. I don't always think that's a wise choice—especially for people who were, for instance, art history or philosophy majors. Somehow I can't help but have the feeling that someday they'll regret not having pursued what they were really interested in.

Counselor Comment

Pat's willingness to do volunteer work soon after graduation was a smart move. She knew instinctively what it takes others a long time to discover—that staying close to your desired field is essential to making contacts and gaining experience, even if you're not being paid for what you want to do.

In contemplating a move to Italy, Pat's sense of risk-taking is alive and well. She travels from one situation to another with the normal fears, but with an underlying confidence that she will find or create good opportunities for herself. Pat relies upon her writing skill, her versatility, and her interpersonal skills. She will not have a straight-line career, but she will be creative enough to use her skills in new situations. Her desire to risk, travel, and bounce around will make her a career adventurer and that adaptability will make her attractive to future employers.

The Present: Patricia Torres now works for Hoover, Berg, Desmond, an architectural firm, as marketing director. She has held this job for three and a half years and loves it and the people she works with. Pat is also on the city council in Littleton, Colorado.

KATHY ENGLE
Account Executive - AT&T
Major - English

At Dickinson I majored in English and minored in French and was active in theatre and dance. I was the product of a slightly spoiled upbringing and had no realistic attitude about "working" after college.

After graduation, I had no specific goals or desires except to perhaps somehow utilize my dance and theatrical training. I moved to Boston, waitressed in several rock nite clubs, signed up with a modeling agency and worked part-time at modeling, and then auditioned with a rock band organizer. He set me up as a lead singer with a rock group, and I sang and danced at Nantucket, Worcester, and other areas around Boston.

The summer of '73, two years after I graduated from Dickinson, I broke off a romance in Boston, decided to move back near my parents in Harrisburg, PA, and to do something "serious". (I went through that stage at 23 where I felt I was too "old" to continue performing and time in which to establish a serious career was running out.)

Besides having a desire to perform, I also wanted to be the great social worker; to help people. Thus, back in Harrisburg, I worked as a job development specialist for a leading social service agency. During my year there I made a lot of contacts in the social service field and was on the Advisory Council for the Tri-County Manpower Program. I was a speaker at the 1974 Pennsylvania Governor's Conference on Employment of the Handicapped, and I was elected a member and consequently an officer on the Board of the Addictive Disease Clinic of Harrisburg.

Through my connections, I eventually was offered a position as a job developer with the CETA Mass-Power Program. After two years in this position, I was disenchanted with "helping" others; was suffering from "burn-out."

At Dickinson, I had become interested in studying "health foods" and vegetarianism so, in 1976, I left my job and left Pennsylvania to travel to Florida where I worked at a natural foods health resort and attended classes on diet, exercise, fasting, and other proper living habits. The experience had a very positive impact on my life, and since then I have followed fairly closely the principles I learned there. That experience lasted the summer, and then I moved to the family summer home in Ocean City, New Jersey to live near the sea, which I felt was more healthful.

The idea of working for a college intrigued me because I love a learning environment, so I was hired by Atlantic Community College as an administrative assistant in the Cape May County Center to develop special programs for Senior citizens, women, and others.

During this time, I was elected an officer for the Cape May County Interagency Council, elected to a 3-year term as delegate to Cape May Title XX Human Services Coalition and eventually as delegate to the State Advisory Council. I also received the "Outstanding Young Woman of the Year Award" by the Cape May Jaycee-ettes.

After three years at the college, however, I was becoming extremely frustrated at not getting enough administrative support and not getting paid what I thought I was worth. So I decided to look elsewhere.

Through raising other women's consciousness to get into non-traditional fields at my workshops, I decided business was "where it was at" for women. If you performed well, at least they would pay you for it. I went through the employment routine with Bell Tel, for which the procedure was long and rigorous for the position I wanted: account executive. Then, in April 1980, I entered the world of business, something very different from the jobs I previously held. For the first six months I received intensive training in technical equipment and business problems and financial analysis. I love the job, have a lot of independence, and constant challenge. I get to utilize my "people" skills from social work, my acting skills from my theatrical background, and my logic, math, and business acumen.

Although most of the rising "stars" at AT&T have business background and usually MBA's, I'm glad I have a liberal arts background—I would do it again!

As for the future—many things are possible. I can see myself having a successful career in marketing at AT&T. I'd also like to write a book, probably a biography about an interesting English character of the Victorian Era. My open-mindedness keeps me living day by day.

Counselor Comment

The desire to have many different careers, or perhaps do several things at the same time, often plagues the liberal arts graduate. However, Kathy Engle has made a virtue of this. She moved from the entertainment field to social service to business, without breaking stride. Kathy recognized over time that her "liberal skills" cut across many different kinds of work, and she learned to apply them in the field, and will use her prior skills and experiences wherever she may go. Kathy provides support for the idea that "nothing you do is ever wasted".

She applies her entertainment background as a public speaker, her social service background in terms of understanding and helping the people she supervises, and her educational background helps in training new employees. Her work in business will enhance her versatility, so that she can move in any of several directions in the future.

The Present: Kathy has earned her MBA and now works for the Diamond State Telephone Company as an account executive.

CAROL MERRITT CHESLEY
English Teacher in European Countries
Major - Biology

Although my major was biology, I decided in my senior year that I wanted to try to go to West Germany to teach English. So I wrote lots of letters to German public school systems, most of which elicited negative responses, but several led to other possibilities. I finally received (about 10 months after I first started writing, I might add) a job offer as an English assistant at a high school in Hamburg, and I worked there for one year. After that, I decided to stay in Hamburg and worked for the Berlitz School of Languages for two more years.

At that point, I felt ready to return to the United States, but wanted to travel a bit first, so I headed for Asia via the Trans-Siberian Railroad. Though I thought I was on my way home, I ended up spending two years in Japan. My first year I again taught English, this time primarily to Japanese children. Tired of teaching, I worked for a short time as a salesperson for World Book Encyclopedia (of all things!) before going back to the English school as an assistant director. This job, which I very much enjoyed, I held for a year before returning to the U.S.. With the director, I was responsible for hiring, training, and supervision of a teaching staff of 20. I also did a lot of work in researching and developing new teaching programs. (This is beginning to sound like a resume!) The program I spent most of my last 6 months working on—a course on how to teach English to children—will be published as a book next year in Japan. Because it was a very small organization, I was able to get involved in many different minor projects, such as translations, recording, and sign language for the deaf.

I have been back in Washington now since early October, and am hoping to find a job as a research assistant for a consulting firm or an association of some sort. So in many ways, I am actually rather like your current liberal arts graduate, wondering how "marketable" I am.

It's difficult to analyze the effect, if any, my Dickinson education had on my post-graduate drifting. I didn't pursue my major area of study, nor do I have any plans to. I always viewed my college education as an education and not as career training.

I'm still wondering if this is a success story or not...!

Counselor Comment

At this point of this letter, Merritt is struggling, wondering what will happen next. Her work experiences abroad developed several key skill areas—teaching, writing, training, language facility, and sensitivity to other cultures. These skills will work greatly in her favor as she seeks new jobs and a new career direction. Her experience in other countries could be of interest to either profit or nonprofit organizations. She will probably recombine her skills and interests in a different way, and will once again discover that she is "marketable".

The Present: Carol is once again in Japan, this time as Assistant Agricultural Attachee (economist) with the US Embassy in Tokyo.

ED WEISS
Labor - Management Relations / Law Student
Majors - Economics and Judaic Studies

What an adventure, trying to figure out what noble (and ignoble, eh?) Dickinsonians are doing with the gifts of Dickinson! In any event, here are some of my impressions.

Let me use Dickinson as a base for the analysis or narrative. At the Prep (Dickinson) I majored in three, no four, things: economics, Judaic studies, working (for pay), and having some fun. However, only the first will be dealt with here. At the Prep, I read some Marx and I think that stuck with me more than anything else in economics. I did some math and the methodology may have crept into my problem solving approach. On second thought, I will also deal with my jobs at the Prep; they definitely helped me to realize how to cope with and perhaps manipulate organizations while also only beginning to open my eyes to looking into other people to see their needs, ideas, etc. In both economics and my jobs, I was able to be a fairly independent operator, e.g. a lot of independent studies.

All of these elements weave through my professional life to this day and will persist for at least the foreseeable future.

I went to grad school right after the Prep (that's one reason why I call it Prep; another is that I still wear penny loafers, although I think I don't like them). Grad work intensified my labor and econ credentials. Also, I really think a major reason for going to grad school was that Dickinson was a womb and I was not confident that I had any marketable skills. To the positive, I often loved learning at the Prep and wanted some more of it.

After grad school, I taught two labor courses at Dickinson and worked with the community manpower programs. These ventures were time bidding efforts, as I look back. I wanted to work directly in the field of labor-management relations and could find no work, so I took what was available and respectable.

I came to Washington and began my labor-management career. The real bridge here was grad school to Washington, the jobs in Carlisle after grad school being interludes. The subject matter I have used is all from grad school. Much of the problem solving is the street smarts that high school in the intercity taught me with a measure added at the Prep. The independence is a rub here in the Bureaucracy and is the reason why I'm pursuing a profession.

Now I am in law school at night, working by day. The mandella keeps turning and I am not sure that I will ever get off it. I still like "school". I had that value before the Prep, and it may have nurtured it a bit. The Prep's ambience still encourages me (inspires is too strong a word.) I may always stay close to academe for professional and personal reasons. I also believe the Prep in the last 60's imbued me with the egotism that I can change things and change is often impossible in the federal government.

I anticipate a patchwork career ahead of me—as singular goals not merely the (vain??) pursuit of satisfying and meaningful and remunerative work. Is that the renaissance? Is that liberal education still playing with my head? Is that the 1960's aversion to acceptance of responsibility or hard/fast rules? Maybe in ten years, I'll know more.

Counselor Comment

The reflections of a graduate of the 60's are evident here. Ed has grown, learned, and acquired important experiences, and can probably succeed at many different careers, but he wonders about his place in the big picture and speculates about the choices he has made in his life. Perhaps he will always question whether his career direction was the right one. And he may have less "success" in conventional terms than a graduate who had barreled straight ahead. But perhaps this is "success" in a deeper sense, a willingness to evaluate what you are doing in societal terms and an ongoing search for work that makes a difference. I suspect that Ed is a little too critical in assessing his career. He gives a lot and expects a lot of himself, yet is not obsessed with self-importance. He is probably too pessimistic about his career prospects. He may never care to "make it" in the ways that others do, but he has enough intelligence, breadth of vision, and concern about social issues to be of great value to many different organizations. I would expect him to become a leader in public or community service, once his formal education and career meanderings are completed.

The Present: Ed is now an Associate Attorney with Foley, Hoag, and Eliot. Still has some funny remarks.

JOHN SANTORO
Manager - Editorial Services
Major - Political Scienc

I went to work immediately after college for Brecker and Merryman, a company that produces literature for major corporations that they use to recruit college graduates. On the creative side, I'm responsible for conceptualizing, researching, and writing recruitment brochures and working with artists, editors, photographers, and clients to make these brochures a printed reality...My interviews bring me in contact with esoteric research scientists, hard-headed executives, junior trainees, and corporate CEO's. I learned a great deal about interviewing as part of my liberal education. This training helps me to establish a rapport with my subjects, and I can probably discuss something of interest with each one of them. Writing a recruiting brochure means taking the sum of your knowledge about the company and distilling it into a memorable and readable text. This skill is probably the greatest benefit of my education. I learned enough about writing to get me the job and to keep me successful in it. Given the general decline of writing skills in our country, people who learn to write—and write well—will be in demand, just as computer operators, electrical engineers, and plumbers are in short supply.

Working with other individuals also harnesses my liberal education. I work well with artists and photographers because I understand their perspectives. The liberal education, with exposure to many different kinds of disciplines and people, offers an advantage over a narrow specialty where you are likely to work with and learn from experts in a narrower range of fields.

Let's look at the second side of my job, the management side. I have to manage the activities of 10 or so people...Good interpersonal skills are a key to good management, and my liberal arts background definitely built my interpersonal skills. The ability to listen, gather information, and solve problems with that information is a skill that was largely honed and built in college."

Counselor Comment

As he neared graduation, John knew that he had writing talent, but he had little idea of where he could apply it in the working world. He had been sports editor of the college newspaper, but did not want journalism. He soon learned that writing skills were needed in private industry as well as government and nonprofit organizations. Through contacts, he met Dick Brecker and was offered a job in New York, allowing him to be near his family in New Jersey. John's work at Brecker and Merryman became a blend of writing and management, as he assumed greater responsibility. The liberal skills - analytical thinking, interpersonal effectiveness, imagination, and judgement - became increasingly important as he took on supervisory and managerial roles. Writing skill gained John the entry he needed, and the broader array of skills enabled him to advance. His work with the spectrum of major corporations covers many different kinds of technical products and services. He learns quickly about any topic, and is comfortable conversing with people in any type of job.

The Present: John is still with Brecker and Merryman but has been promoted to Director of Creative Services.

STEVE PARKER
Occupation - Farrier (Blacksmith)
Majors - Biology and Economics

"I'll bet my presence at Dickinson has hardly been missed since my graduation except for the collective sigh of relief from my defeated professors. Good men all, but not really up to the challenge, I'm afraid. I've become a blue-collar celebrity of sorts. Imagine, a local horseshoer with a B.S. in Biology and Economics. Rather titillates the fancy of over-and under-educated people alike.

I am given to reflections and gentle musings from time to time on the nature of man, the understanding of happiness, etc.. And long before you suggested the topic, I had weighed the pros and cons of a liberal arts education. How is one to separate one's own talents, interests, ideas, predilections, strengths, i.e. natural attributes from the exposure and polish of four years of liberal arts eduction? Am I not the same person today that I was four years ago?

I'll answer that. I'm very much the same person, but just as the successful marathon runner is strengthened by rigors of training, so have I benefitted from the rigors of four years of liberal arts education. That, combined with my natural tenacity, gives me the skill to be successful at anything I put my hand to. Attitude is the one prerequisite for success and a liberal arts education can give you an attitude of quiet confidence.

I am a successful farrier because I can read, write, and express myself to all levels of understanding. I can communicate to people without condescending or offending them. I can hold my own with the high-brow who has a plunging charger in the back yard. The skill is born of education and is probably more important in the definition of my success than in my skill at shoeing a horse! It's true, and I suspect the skill of communication weaves through the success of people and careers universally.

P.S. - I'm working on some crustacean research that may yield $millions. If is does, I'll really endorse a liberal arts education, as the seeds of this project were planted in an invertebrate zoology class years ago.

Counselor Comment

The word "career" derives from a French word meaning "to race around a track". Steve Parker took this word more literally than most in developing his chosen work.

Steve had the gumption to make his career as a farrier, because this is what he wanted to do most. Would a business major become a blacksmith? I doubt it. There is too much social norming in business school toward making money in conventional ways. Steve Parker has done it his way. Steve's career is just one more example which shows that a college education is not "vocational training". But it is a background that enhances one's work, whether it happens to be in an office building or a stable.

The Present: Steve is still shoeing horses. In fact he was calling from a barn when he gave permission to use his comments. He gave his permission and asked when his first royalty check would be coming in.

JAN AGNEW
Owner, Advertising Agency
Major - English

"Ten jobs, one marriage, one child, one divorce, hundreds of mistakes, and thousands of learning experiences since the day I left my alma mater, I have opened my own advertising agency in Lancaster, Pennsylvania. The big question, upon graduation, was "What in the world do you do with an English degree if you don't want to teach?" What you do not do with an English degree is take any old job, just because it pays well... After working as an employment agency counselor, health careers coordinator, a customer service correspondent and several other "this -looks-alright-so-I'll-take-it" positions, I figured it was time to start doing what I really wanted to do — write.

"Experience, we want someone with experience," they all said, with hardly a glance at my cherished poetry, college term papers, five-act play, and school newspaper articles.

All together now, liberal arts graduates of America: "But how do we get experience if no one will hire us?"

The solution to that problem for me was the back door approach. You take one very big gulp, swallow your pride, and get your foot right in the door of the business you'd most like to make your career in. That could mean starting out as a mail clerk, some dimwit's secretary, or an assistant to an assistant... In the business world, it's called paying your dues.

Soon after I moved to Lancaster, I noticed a little ad in the Classified section of the local newspaper. I remember exactly what it said:

> *START YOUR CAREER IN ADVERTISING. Begin with secretarial and*
> *bookkeeping duties, then move into media, scheduling, production - anything*
> *you have the talent and energy to learn.*

I sat behind that typewriter for two months and learned through osmosis what the ad agency business was about. I typed hundred of pages of other people's copy and then realized "Hey, I can do this for sure." I brought in all my best writing samples I could gather, plopped them on the president's desk, and three days later I was a copywriter! The months went by and I began to realize that fewer and fewer of my copy assignments were being returned for re-writes. At last, I had "experience" and I had no trouble at all getting a position as a promotion supervisor in the advertising and marketing department of a world-wide manufacturer of floors, ceilings, and carpets — Armstrong World Industries. The two years I spent at Armstrong were like going to graduate school. I worked with interior designers, photographers, artists, media specialists, and production experts, all the people who were responsible for producing those gorgeous four-color national magazine ads.

In my particular type of business, a liberal arts education was important, It gave me an open mind and a keen interest to always learn more. That is definitely a virtue in advertising. Every day I learn something new about somebody else's business—whether it's banking or real estate or giftware or restaurants or architectural stone. I must open my mind to the efforts of my clients' businesses, understand them, and communicate their selling points to the trade and consumers.

Counselor Comment
No college graduate should expect the pieces to fall into place from the start, and Jan Agnew's story is testament to that. But her doggedness about the writing profession, and her willingness to be a neophyte, paid off. She cling to her belief that she had talent and found the right avenues to gain experience and display her wares. She refined her skills and developed the necessary toughness along the way. Jan struggled early, but what seemed to be a hodge-podge of jobs was providing her the diversity of experience that would help her to better understand a wide range of advertising clientele. Jan's sense of humor helped her through the hard times and allowed her to see temporary setbacks as part of the larger picture of her personal growth.

The Present: Jan is president of her own company, Agnew and Corrigan, and also serves as Creative Director for this $7 million a year advertising agency.

RODNEY KEEFER
Policy Officer
Major - Psychology

"I had several summer jobs during college as a Y-camp counselor. After college, I went into the military police corps in the Army... I found the Army life both frustrating and rewarding. After the two-year stint, I joined the Fairfax County Police Department in Virginia. College grads, I think, make better cops, and are welcomed by the administration... Police work is primarily counseling those persons who, for one reason or another, have allowed themselves to create problems where none existed before. I enjoy assisting people who are in genuine need. The liberal arts college with requirements in different fields of endeavor has made getting along with people from all walks of life a much more stimulating experience and a lot less hassle.

Counselor Comment
Who else but a liberal arts graduate would perceive police work as "primarily counseling" and "assisting people who are in genuine need"? Since when do camp counselors become police officers? When they view human service as an opportunity to affect how others view their lives. The larger, social perspective may help Rod Keefer get past the jagged edges of police work. One would think that police administrators like liberal arts graduates because they view their work as something more than a contest between cops and robbers.

The Present: Rodney is still with the Fairfax County Police Department but is now a plain clothes detective.

JUDY LA BARRE
Project Work/Environmental Engineering
Major - Chemistry

"I'm afraid I don't have a very exciting story for you. After graduation I went to work at Chilton Publishing for a trade journal called __Food Engineering__. Leaving school with a chemistry major, a secondary education minor, and work on the (Dickinsonian), I wanted to try something combining science and journalism... The main reward (on the job) was David —we both worked on the magazine. Well, he was transferred to Chicago and as the phone and plane bills mounted, we decided to get married. Meanwhile, he got a job with Ralston at Checkerboard Square, St. Louis (there really is a Checkerboard Square) so I left Chilton after one year. Now David had a great new job with lots of promise, so it was my turn to find something—anything, to make money at first... I was ready to try waitressing (remember I had four years food service experience) when I saw an ad for part-time

work at an environmental firm... Since I've been here I've done lab work, worked on environmental impact statements, done some library research, had contact with clients and assisted them with governmental regulations and permits, and done a lot of data reporting. Since it is a small company, I've had a chance to do a lot of different things. These days I do mostly small project management and data management. I think my Dickinson background has been helpful in giving me diverse skills and interests.

I'll be working at least until we have more kids. And, if we have another, I won't be able to afford to quit!

Counselor Comment

The cross-currents of Judy's family life and work life are apparent. She is highly intelligent, has superior interpersonal skills, and was editor of her college newspaper. Perhaps she could be doing more career-wise if she were not devoting considerable energy to being a mother. On the other hand, her technical background and diversity of job assignments are giving her the foundation for a number of different leadership roles, if she wants them. Technical skills and communication skills are a powerful combination. Judy will decide how much career responsibility she wants. Her talents can be useful to corporations, government agencies, consulting firms, and research-development organizations.

The Present: Judy LaBarre Stone is now working as a project manager for Weston Analytics, an environmental consulting firm.

CAROLYN BOURDOW
Attorney
Major - Psychology

"After graduation I taught a semester in a school for pregnant junior and senior high school students... then I taught a full year in a rural high school, teaching US history and government, and eighth-grade social studies. I had a hard time getting used to being a "performer" —constantly acting to try to stimulate the large classes of (mostly) bored high school students, most of whom seemed burnt out after 11 or 12 years of school. At any rate, I learned a lot that year and was surprised when I was awarded a plaque from the graduating senior class as their most "outstanding teacher." I had already told the principal I would not be returning. I just didn't feel down deep that teaching was for me. While sort of floundering around, I came up with the crazy idea of making educational materials for public schools. I decided to make materials on Virginia history since Virginia, chauvinistic state that it is, requires teachers to teach units in Virginia history in at least three different grades. Anyway, Dominion Media Company was born. I worked with DMC full-time for a year, before finding myself drawn to law school, and the business operated part-time during my three years of law school, at least to the extent of paying for school. I really guess it was the setting up of the business that gave me the immediate push to try law school. I remember going to a local attorney friend of mine in Staunton to find out how to copyright my programs. Marshall (who not, incidentally, is Attorney General of Virginia, and loves to repeat this story) said he really didn't know but that if I came back in a week he would have all the information. He charged me $97.50. Anyway, I ended up in U. of Virginia law school and three years later was in private practice in Richmond.

If I had to come up with one "tool" I picked up at Dickinson, it would have to be "curiosity." I can never get over the feeling of the vastness of the world and all that there is to learn and know... After eight years, it's still too early to draw many conclusions for myself—I still feel like I am part of an evolution, and really have no clear feeling of where I'll be five or ten years from now. I do think I got some good building blocks at Dickinson to take with me on this evolution.

Counselor Comment

During college, there was little clue that Carolyn had the talent or inclination to become a lawyer. She stayed out of politics, kept a low profile, and involved herself mostly in community service. Her versatility did not surface until after graduation. The Dominion Media Company was a clear tipoff that Carolyn had little fear of applying her intelligence and education to any field of work, no matter how unfamiliar it might be. I suspect this was a combined result of Carolyn's risk-taking nature and the confidence inspired by her general education. At Dickinson, Carolyn's most notable contribution was single-handed coordination of the campus crisis-intervention hotline called Night Owl, under the supervision of the college psychologist. It was interesting, but perhaps not surprising, to see this intensity and dedication shift to business and legal after graduation.

The Present: Carolyn is now an attorney with the law firm of Bourdow and Bowen.

WEETIE COHO
Controller - Manager/Volvo Dealership
Major - American Studies

"My parents felt a college education was worth the time and effort if only to enable me to speak intelligently at dinner parties... Dickinson did send us out into the working world with opinions of our worth that were perhaps too elevated. I was insulted that my first job offered so little money. That job lasted nine months. It was an accounting position as assistant comptroller for five retail record corporations. My second and last job was as comptroller/business manager for a Volvo dealership. My second and third years in this job, I was ranked #1 nationally for Volvo franchise business managers.

My Dickinson education gave me no specifics that led to my career (I never took accounting), but it did give me the time and guidance to mature and enhance my comprehension of the world. I have absolutely no complaints about Dickinson and would not trade my four years for anything.

Counselor Comment

Some business people like to claim that you must take the right courses in order to perform in their world, but individuals like Weetie Coho show that general intelligence and motivation can get the job done too. Liberal arts is not simply a pursuit of all those subjects which are non-vocational. It is the development of mental faculties that enable a graduate to learn new material, grasp new concepts, and integrate this learning with practical demands.

The Present: Weetie has been home raising her three children the past eight years. She does a lot of volunteer work and has been involved with Cub Scouts, teaching math at school, etc.. Also a bit involved in politics; at this writing her brother is running for Lt. Governor, Virginia.

AUSTIN BURKE
Director of Economic Development, Scranton, PA
Major - Economics

"The first requirement for the job of selling Scranton is a sense of humor. Granted, a liberal arts education does not necessarily include HUMOR 101, however, it does give a broader view of the world so that we can keep our day to day problems in perspective. Perhaps this is the greatest advantage of a liberal education... After graduation I went into research for the non-profit Economic Development Council of Northeastern Pennsylvania. There I gravitated toward the development end of the job, first providing background research, and then grooming the proposals and selling them to the appropriate government financing agencies. This was a people-oriented job that provided a

nice mix of interesting concepts and projects and good contacts with private and government "big wheels." A new executive vice-president at the Scranton Chamber of Commerce offered me the chance to do even more development through five different subsidiaries which do everything from industrial parks and buildings to downtown development and even working capital loans to small businesses. It's a great job —sometimes we meet the captains of industry and finance, sometimes we meet con men (sometimes they're the same people)...

The Dickinson liberal arts education provided the confidence and background to meet a variety of people with different backgrounds and different goals. Familiarity with a broad range of disciplines gave me a more fertile environment for the appropriate consideration and solution of complex and sometimes contradictory problems.

Counselor Comment

Perhaps you are thinking, as I am, that Austin would have made it in his career, regardless of what he had studied in college. Maybe so, but I also believe him when he says that a broad education helped him to encounter high-powered executives, farmers, and government officials alike. In the field of economic development, Austin must no doubt appreciate the relationships between politics, science/technology, the history of a region, the sociology of population patterns, the languages of people who settle from other countries, and the psychology of selling a city to potential investors.

The Present: Austin now works for the Chamber of Commerce in Archbald, PA.

What Do These Letters Reveal?

What do we learn by reading the stories of these liberal arts graduates, not long after their departures from a campus? Are there any lessons for today's graduate who faces similar situations?

(1) Initial Struggle

The years immediately after graduation are sometimes difficult, in that good jobs do not come easily and the grads change their minds about what they want to do. They have periods of doubt and/or unemployment, and they suffer personal or financial setbacks. However, almost without fail, they emerge from the uncertainties as stronger people who have a lot of abilities, and eventually develop focus in their careers.

They use many different techniques in launching their career and gaining the experience that will help them compete for advancement and determine, for themselves, how well they like and perform certain roles. They may get this experience from part-time work while in school, from volunteer work, or from temporary jobs.

Often initial work is followed up with advanced training related to their emerging career goals.

(2) A Willingness to Question Themselves

If a liberal education did not exist, these people would have invented it. The "curiosity" and instinct toward self-reflection is apparent in most of the letters. These grads do not see a career as an orderly process, but rather a thing that must be examined and re-examined. They wonder aloud about how their jobs and careers fit into the world and how their work fits with the rest of their lives.

(3) A Concern With More Than Bottom Lines

Money, status, power, and "getting ahead" seldom are given prominent attention in how these graduates view their work. Despite being in uncertain financial states, their concerns focus on how interesting the work is, opportunity to apply their talents, and contribution to others.

Their enthusiasm for life and their willingness to step up and take risks to make significant gains must be admired. Their total life pattern often involves an interesting job, a chance to explore new parts of the country or the world, and community service activities.

(4) A Sense of Humor

Several graduates poke indirect and gentle fun at the overly serious enterprise of Work. Not wanting to get caught in the swirling vortex of Career Achievement, they step aside and view the cultural imperative to "get ahead" with some

"The attributes of liberal arts graduates rated most highly by employers are writing, public speaking, management supervision, reading and interpretation, and public relations."

Michigan State University Placement Service report

bemusement. Rather than accept the "competition" theme of careerism and join the game, they create their own games with different rules.

They found resources to bounce back after adversity and to take a long view of life rather than get depressed about short term problems. This helped them move easily into a variety of situations—some dead end and others offering promise for the future.

(5) Ability to Listen and Learn

Education does not end with graduation from college and the graduates found that every situation was a learning experience. Each job required the acquisition of specific information and a new set of contacts.

People are an important part of the learning process. All jobs present interpersonal challenges and learning how to work with those around you is often the single most important key to success. Working is understanding customers, colleagues, and others. Working is also trying to understand what they are saying and their needs and goals.

(6) A Quiet Confidence

Beneath the immediate struggles and uncertainties, most grads reveal a belief that they will eventually forge their own directions and achieve success, in both conventional terms and according to their own criteria. Even when unemployed or under-employed, they do not despair or panic. The worst one might say is that "I have not found my particular direction yet (but I know that I will)."

Their confidence has helped them successfully cope with challenges in all parts of the world, to compete for jobs with success, and to keep their heads high and their hopes on the upbeat.

"Diverse interests led to much career confusion and indecision, an inability to focus and specialize. On the positive side, my broad background gave me confidence I could successfully perform in any job I desired."

University of Texas graduate

Are These Grads Successful or Not?

In their beginning career years, as depicted in these letters, these graduates might not view themselves as "successful." Clearly it is too early to make that judgment. Bringing matters up to the present, in terms of their present job or career titles, they have considerable success, as measured by status, income earned, and variety of their work roles. However, these grads would undoubtedly evaluate themselves by different standards. They would ask: "Is my work making a difference to others?", "How much am I growing in this career?", "Does my work affect my family life positively?", "Am I using all of my abilities?", and other such questions. Success, to these graduates, is defined by the individual, according to how they place themselves in the larger societal context.

Would You Want Your Career To Develop The Way Theirs Have?

Perhaps the trials, hitches, and occasional discombobulation of careers that occurred for these liberal arts graduates is more discomfort than you would want. Maybe you would want your progress form college to the job world to be more orderly and your advancement more predictable. If so, you are going to miss some of the beauty of career development - applying your abilities to new fields, to jobs you did not learn about in college. Bouncing around and feeling your way and learning a job from the ground up may have their uncomfortable moments, but real careers are more like that than the lock-step, career ladder progressions that everyone hopes for. You might as well get used to it. Careers cannot be mapped in advance. The letters from these grads are typical, and their ability to cope with the unevenness is a compliment to both themselves and to the versatility they derived from their liberal education.

"The qualities in young executives which appeal to me are honesty, candor, good judgement, intelligence, imagination, and the ability to write clear, concise memos."

Henry Ford II
Industrialist

28

What Research Studies Conclude About Liberal Arts

Analyzing the research on liberal education and careers the following themes emerge.

(1) Liberal Arts Graduates are Found Across the Entire Landscape of the World of Work.

Business is by no means the sole province of business graduates. Liberal arts alumni are there in abundance as they are also found in government, community agencies, colleges, foundations, human service groups and most everywhere else as well. The majority of these liberal arts graduates obtained their positions without having to earn additional degrees.

(2) Liberal Learning is More Important in the Longer Run and Less Salable Initially.

Organizations may hire initially to get technical skills but they are also looking for long-range managerial talent. Businesses are starting to question their addiction to short-run profits and are coming to see the importance of the longer view. This awakening among business leaders is leading them to give greater attention to hiring graduates who think broadly and have vision.

(3) The Liberal Arts Graduate Definitely Belongs in the Vast World of Computers.

The analytical skills of liberal arts graduates make them welcome in roles as systems analysts and in the application of computer skills to organizational problems.

(4) High Tech Organizations Have an Abundant Need for Liberal Arts Graduates.

As Levin and Rumberger have noted most jobs in high tech firms are non-technical. Similar evidence is presented in the **High Tech Career Guide** and in **High Tech Jobs For Non Tech Grads.**

(5) Business Executives Repeatedly State that Academic Specialization is not Necessary for Success in Business.

Many of them make this comment because they, themselves, came from a strong background in liberal education. Some of them are quoted in this book.

(6) There are Numerous Specific Foundational Skills that Tend to be Associated with a Liberal Education.

Examples here include thinking, writing, research, analytical reasoning, foreign language facility, public discourse, and critique. All of these skills are transferable from one job to another, from one industry to another, and from one level of responsibility to higher levels.

"I have observed time and time again those who are able to express themselves clearly and simply—either spoken or written word—move ahead more rapidly."

Hamline University graduate

"Education does not stop with graduation from college. I read a number of periodicals and three or four good books each month. Education is only a ticket to a full like, not an all-expenses guided tour."

Miami University graduate

(7) Liberal Arts Graduates are at Least as Successful as Their Counterparts in Other Disciplines and Often are More Successful in Terms of Advancement and Earnings When Long-Range Studies are Conducted.

Research done by AT&T and the Chase Manhattan Bank support this long-run view of the values of liberal education. However, additional research would be helpful.

(8) Many Present Organizational Leaders have a Liberal Arts Background.

A Forbes study focused on this evidence. Many of the firms who responded continue to look to liberal arts graduates as a rich source of future leadership.

(9) The Skills of Liberal Learning and the Skills of an Effective Manager, in Both Profit and Non-Profit Organizations, are Closely Connected.

Interpersonal skills are viewed as being perhaps the key to executive success. Nobody wants a manager who understands financial transactions but cannot motivate people and cannot handle conflicts with co-workers or superiors.

(10) There is Considerable Evidence that the Liberal Arts Degree is Highly Versatile.

Liberal arts can help in many different ways, often unseen at the beginning. A music major, for example, may see a vacancy in market research and wonder how he or she is supposed to qualify. First of all, a music major may have some mathematical ability as musical notation is mathematical in its concepts. More importantly, the graduate makes it his or her business to read about survey and research methods, does a little review on the products and services of the employer, and tells the organization, "I can handle this job, just give me a chance."

The point is not that music majors make good market researchers but rather that skills needed in this job, or any job, often can be found and cultivated by many college graduates — regardless of their specific academic background.

(11) Liberal Arts Graduates are Appreciated for Their Adaptablitity.

They can use their general learning skills to work with previously unfamiliar problems. When a publishing company acquires an electronic music business, it wants the managing editor (a liberal arts geology major) to learn the electronic music trade and understand its issues without skipping measure.

(12) There is a Tremendous Need for Strong Writing Skills and Employers Appreciate Managers who can Produce Effective Memoranda and Reports.

Liberal arts graduates are highly prized for their abilities to express complex concepts in clear language that others can understand.

(13) There is Increasing Concern that Business Education is too Narrow for the Employer's Own Good.

Many feel that a broader vision of liberal education is needed to help business deal with its international and long-range problems.

Upper level executives see the unintended effects of selection decisions made by lower level managers. The business school graduate is adequately trained to get the first job but often has difficulty holding it and advancing. Business education, which is primarily fact-oriented, often is an accumulation of solutions to yesterday's problems. The rate at which the world changes prevents schools from keeping their curricula current.

(14) Technological Literacy is Increasingly Important For Liberal Arts Graduates.

They must make computers, science, mathematics, and related technological concerns part of their liberal education if they expect to understand and compete in the modern world. While business admires the general literacy of the liberal arts graduate, it cannot tolerate a graduate who is unfamiliar with technical ideas or unwilling to talk in technical language.

(15) It is Clear that Liberal Arts Graduates have more Difficulty Landing Their First Jobs than Their Specialized Counterparts.

This is because they are making a transition from broad academic learning to the very focused needs of the marketplace. For a while, liberal arts graduates may be stunned. They don't know what kind of work they want or how to sell themselves and their degree, but once they overcome these hurdles, and this is easily possible, they can develop a career focus and compete effectively in the job market.

"The most magnificantly trained doctor can actually be injurious to our psychological well-being; technical competence cannot compensate for human indifference."

"Dirty Words: Leadership and Liberal Learning"

<u>*Change Magazine*</u>*, April 1980*

CAREER PROFILE

"Employers won't care what degree you have if you can do the job. The bottom line is 'Can you get the job done?'"

Mark Longley
BA, Humanities, 1981
Now a publications coordinator

Liberal Arts Education

Certain skills are transferable from college to the work world, like managing your time, meeting deadlines, being able to make and change plans, and being able to anticipate and solve problems. As a nondepartmental major at U.T. I had to design and follow my own curriculum, so I had to be independent, broadminded and farsighted to keep from wasting time and money. I learned to manage myself.

Certain courses have been valuable to me; my language studies helped me to learn to deal with a variety of people. (I use people skills a lot now in dealing with phone calls and with my fellow employees). English and composition allowed me to practice writing skills; and computer science would later help me learn to use real world computers quickly.

Job Search Techniques/Results

While attending U.T. I got hooked into a couple of key teachers who were familiar with the business I wanted to get into —publishing, editing, and writing. I managed to find extra coursework in editing and writing, and I took a lot of hard science courses that gave me a broad grounding in the different areas I wanted to work in— science and mathematics. I talked to people working with publications, magazines, books—every from of published material—and about midway through college I managed to get a job as an editorial assistant. As an editorial assistant in a small editorial house on campus. I did mechanical things to prepare publications—paste-up and typesetting. Eventually I started doing the same things for a larger publishing company which published books and materials for the petroleum industry. When I graduated they hired me as an editor. I ended up writing two books for them, two manuals, and editing a lot of materials—anything from brochures to teacher's manuals.

I eventually quit when the petroleum industry started to contract and put together a portfolio emphasizing all of the things I had done. A publisher of computer use magazines hired me as an editor. In this job I had to make a lot of managerial decisions such as who's going to do what work, when will it be ready, when are things going to come together for other departments to work with and so on.

Publishing a technical magazine, my editorial staff and I served as information buffers for people who need information in their daily businesses; we had to keep on top of things and be prepared to answer a lot of questions.

In my current job, I serve as publications coordinator for a research center. We have a lot of visitors who attend staff presentations, and our researchers travel a great deal to inform others of our work and to exchange ideas. These activities involve the handling of much information in many combinations and forms—presentations, conference papers, reports, proposals, and brochures—according to the needs of the targeted audience. It takes the same management skills I've used to keep all the irons hot, and the same people skills to help everyone cool and confident no matter how high the heat rises. This kind of work environment requires the ability—and willingness— to shift gears as needed, something I first learned as an interdisciplinary liberal arts major.

Job Advice

Find people in the profession you're looking at, and talk to them. Find out what they've done, what they liked, what they didn't like, what kind of people are in the profession, and try to picture yourself doing that kind of work.

Get a job even if it's a non-paying job. By getting work experience, and by beginning to think of yourself as a professional, you can get a headstart on the job search.

Remember that college is not going to give you a job. All it does is give you a set of attitudes and a set of ideas about work, about how information is used.

A degree is not what makes you marketable. In a certain sense a degree is important, because it shows that you're college educated and that you're willing to put out effort for long-term gratification. Employers won't care what degree you have if you can do the job. The bottom line is, "Can you get the job done well?"

College is the place to find out about your abilities, and it's your abilities that an employer wants to buy. But knowing your abilities isn't enough, you have to know how to apply them. Learning to apply marketable abilities while still in college is a particular challenge for liberal arts majors, but it's one well worth meeting.

Answers to Key Questions Asked by Liberal Arts Students

The decision to major in liberal arts is often not an easy one when the student stops to consider its career implications. While some students take it on faith that the liberal arts degree will lead to suitable career goals many others puzzle over how to translate their liberal education into viable preparation for the world of work. They know that few philosophy majors work as philosophers and most history majors do not get jobs as historians. The transition between liberal studies and a specific occupational focus raises predictable questions. Here is how you can answer some of the most frequently raised questions for yourself.

"The problems of the real world are much more like what you find in Hemingway and Faulkner than what you find in a marketing text."

"What Can You Do with an English Major?"
Journal of College Placement,
Summer 1985.

(1) How do You Answer the Job Interviewer who asks "Why did you Major in Liberal Arts?"

This is one of those big loaded questions. The interviewer really means to ask: "Why didn't you major in business, or some other field of study that would <u>prepare</u> you for a career?". Well, there it is. It's a question that can make you feel quite defensive, but that is not necessary. You can answer in several ways; such as illustrated below:

> a) "I felt that a solid liberal education would be the best possible background for any job or profession, including this one (the one you're applying for), because I have developed strong learning skills, analytical skills, and communication skills that I can use in learning the unique work of your organization."

> b) "I wanted a strong education that would help me in a variety of future jobs, and that would enable me to be flexible in learning new assignments and adapting to changing responsibilities."

> c) "I decided that I could learn more about this particular field of work through practical part-time work experience and internships during college".

"A liberal education prepares a man to fill any post with credit, and to master any subject with facility."

John Cardinal Newman
The Idea of a University

> d) "The liberal arts courses at my college are the most challenging educational programs it offers; I wanted to test myself with the best teachers and sharpen my learning skills with the most demanding courses."

The main idea here is to not be defensive about your liberal arts degree, but rather to value it highly and offer a persuasive rationale for having chosen it. You're not making this up; you're telling the interviewer exactly why you made your choice and feel good about it. If you want to back up your choice with some relevant research, cite AT&T or Chase Manhattan studies noted in this book, which indicate the superior progress made by LAG's in their careers, or other studies listed in Section 11.

If the interviewer presses further and wants to know why you did not take some business courses and, therefore, how can you feel "prepared" to do this kind of work, you can say:

> a) "I have researched the entry-level jobs in your organization, and believe that I can learn them quickly and become a contributing member of your company".
>
> b) "I took some business courses and made sure I got some experience in business during college, in my work as_____."
>
> c) "It seemed more worthwhile to sharpen my analytical skills in liberal arts courses."
>
> d) "I have done a lot of reading about the business world in my spare time, including (names of books and journals you have read recently) and this has helped acquaint me with the kinds of activities which interest you."

No liberal arts graduate can give all of the above answers, because they won't all be true of a given individual. However, choose the ones that apply to you, or cite those which you most believe in, and make your best case for being a good job candidate. Usually, the interviewer wants to know that (1) You believe that you have enough learning skill to handle a variety of assignments, (2) You are seriously motivated toward a career in their area of work, as demonstrated by your out-of-class involvements, part-time work, and/or courses taken outside of liberal arts. Here, it pays to also demonstrate some knowledge about the employer to reflect your particular interest in its organization.

In cases where the interviewer feels that you must have certain "technical" skills to qualify for the job (such as accounting, financial analysis, statistics, science, etc.), you should be prepared to demonstrate that you have acquired some of these skills through your coursework or elsewhere.

(2) "Should I take a Few Business Courses?"

Let's assume you would like to get your job and move ahead in the business world, but you are committed to your liberal arts studies. Many teachers and counselors advise supplementing your program with business courses. Is that a good strategy for you? Generally speaking, it's not a bad idea to include a few "technical" courses in your degree plan, ones which contain specific information (such as principles of accounting) that would help you land an entry-level job. You

"Your employer eventually will judge you more on how much work you can get others to do rather than how much you can do yourself."

Duke University graduate

"The recruitment of a number of companies with which I deal is changing from MBA's to high achiever liberal arts students. These companies are realizing that their problems may be due to technically qualified managers who see the trees but lack the wisdom imparted by the liberal arts to see the forest."

Joan Rothberg,
VP Ted Bates Advertising

36

are likely to have room for them in your program. Even if your school does not offer them, you can take good business courses at other colleges during the summer time, or through a semester away. Another good reason for taking business courses is that some of them emphasize the analytical and communication skills that will help you on the job. In other words, some courses in the business school have the flavor of good "liberal education." Look for the teachers who make their students think and express themselves in writing, class discussion, and on exams.

Other liberal arts students may prefer to disregard business courses, either because you don't believe they are particularly strong at your college, can't work them into your programs, not; or because you simply prefer the liberal arts curriculum. Such students may prefer to get their "preparation for business" by getting business work experience during college. Others would simply say: "I don't need to take these business/technical courses...I can get someone to hire me and will learn on-the-job." Some businesses encourage this kind of confident approach, because they would prefer to train the new graduates themselves.

The final answer to the importance of taking business courses rests with the individual student, because there are so many ways that a liberal arts student can "prepare" for a business career. You should select the combination of academic courses and out-of-class experiences that you believe will make you the best possible job candidate. This combination is not likely to be exactly the same as for your friend across the hall but it will be the best for you.

(3) "What do I Say to my Parents if They Want Me to Get Out of Liberal Arts, but I Want to Stay?"

Parents often have a strong orientation towards "vocational preparation" in college programs. They want to see their children equipped to pursue a specific career, so they can go to work after college and not have to regress into dependence upon them. This viewpoint makes them skeptical of the liberal arts, so they ask the uncomfortable question: "What can you do with that?" If you're sticking to liberal arts, but you are uncertain about your career goal, this may put you in conflict with parents who urge you to transfer to a more "useful" college program. Does that sound familiar?

If you are convinced that the liberal arts program is a better education for you, and you believe that it will provide you sound preparation for your future work (even though you may be unsure what that will be), here are the kinds of responses you can offer to your parents:

> a) "I have compared my courses with those of my friends who are in other fields of study, and I am more challenged by the liberal arts courses. They m a k e me work harder and I will have better learning skills as a result of being in these courses."

b) "I am investigating my career fields now, and it looks as though I will be going into the _____ field. I don't want to transfer to another program, because I know I can get into this field with a liberal arts degree."

c) "I know that our college has a program in the career field that I intend to enter, but I don't like it as well as liberal arts. I will take some courses in that department, but I don't want to major there because I don't like the courses that well. I will also see about getting some work experience in that field, to make me a better job candidate when I graduate."

You can defend your choice of liberal arts in a variety of ways but you will also want to be open to your parents' viewpoint. Why do they believe the business courses are better? What kinds of knowledge do they believe you will acquire that you cannot get in liberal arts? What are their opinions of how best to prepare for a career? If you agree, tell them so. If you have a different view, based on your exposure to business people, advice from counselors, or something you have read, tell them how you have developed your perspective. This is an important dialogue. Your ability to communicate your views to your parents will be an important measure of the strength of your conviction about staying in liberal arts.

4) "Is any Liberal Arts Degree as Good as any Other?"

Some liberal arts degrees sound more vocational than others, such as economics (for business careers), or sociology-psychology (for human service careers), or science (for science careers). How much does it matter what you have studied as a liberal arts graduate? Are some degree programs more marketable than others?

The answer depends upon the career field you intend to enter. If you have goals as scientist, certainly majoring in a science field is essential. If you intend to enter graduate study in biology, you should probably concentrate in that area as an undergraduate.

In the social sciences and the humanities, the relationships to future careers are much less clear. In fact, unless you intend to enter graduate study in one of these disciplines, it is much less important that you have a particular undergraduate major in order to enter a specific field of work. While economics may be good preparation for business, it is not required. History, French, philosophy, Latin, anthropology, and English majors also can qualify for jobs in the business world. Furthermore, it is not necessary to be a sociology or psychology major to obtain a bachelor's level job in the human services.

The label of your major or degree is less important than the skills you acquire from a particular program of study. If philosophy gives you the analytical skills that you want, stick with it. If history sharpens your research skills, and you expect to use these in your future work, then that is the major for you. If it is important to you that you understand another culture and learn its language, then study foreign languages. Employers in a wide variety of fields—advertising, banking, retailing, telecommunications, computer services, sales management, insurance, and many others noted elsewhere in this book—are looking for well-schooled college graduates who are motivated to be in their fields of work. They regard the major fields of study as less important than the overall educational preparation, and they often believe that a well-trained mind can be expected to learn about their field of work, regardless of what courses appear on his/her transcript.

Of course, there are employers who believe otherwise. Some may prefer graduates other than those from liberal arts. Others may think that a particular major in liberal arts is the ideal preparation. However, there is no consensus regarding preferred liberal arts majors, and no particular rationale for thinking that a certain liberal arts degree favors the job-seeker. Most employers believe that the college major is only one item in a much larger array of information important about the college graduate. They prefer to look at the whole picture. By "packaging" your coursework, experiences, and motivations effectively, you can present yourself as a suitable candidate for many different kinds of careers.

5) "How Important is the Rating of My College?"

If you graduate from a high-prestige, well-known college or university, your degree will get a bit of extra attention with some employers. It may get you in the door more easily, and some interviewers will add an extra measure of "potential" onto your scorecard. However, do not expect your degree to do the whole job for you. At best, the quality of your college is but one factor of many.

If your school is less well known, don't worry about it. The main fact is that you will have a degree. This simple credential gives you access to thousands of jobs that would otherwise be closed to you. You are in the same pool with all other college grads. Don't ever believe that your school is less-than some other institution. You are the one applying for the job, not your college. All bachelor's degrees are equal until proven otherwise. If an interviewer has not heard of your school, tell him or her: "My college is a small school with a high-quality reputation in liberal arts. Our graduates have become successful in business, education, government, and a variety of careers." You're pretty safe in making that statement. The reason to say this is to show that you are proud of the degree you have received and believe it has prepared you for successful work in any field.

(6) "How Important is My Grade-point Average?"

For job-hunting purposes, your grade average is probably

"The whole object of education is, or should be, to develop the mind. The mind should be the thing that works. It should be able to pas judgement on events as they arise, make decisions."

Playwright Sherwood Anderson

less important than you think. While some employers will set a grade cutoff as a criterion for entry (notably some campus recruiters, who use it as an artificial screening device), many others are aware that grades are a low-grade predictor of success on the job; therefore they are open to applications from people with low as well as high grades. Employers know that many future leaders of businesses and other organizations will have 2.0 to 2.7 grade-points in their backgrounds.

Let's face it. Fifty percent of your graduating class will fall below the median grade-average. So, by definition, 50% will have "low grades." If you are one of these, don't worry about it. In many cases, the "low grades" person was occupied doing other things, building other skills during college. Or, perhaps you were busy earning money to pay for school. Or, maybe you were just having a good time—but even that builds skills, such as social skills, organizing skills, and an ability to get people to work (or play) with you.

Regardless of your reasons for low grades, there are plenty of other assets in your background that make you a good candidate for the job you want. So, the best way to answer a question such as "Why were your grades so low?", is to say:

> a) I did not want to spend all of my time on studies; instead I was busy with _____, and I felt this helped me develop these skills: _____, _____, and _____.

> b) I wanted to have a diverse experience in college, where I would be involved with people in a variety of ways.

> c) I am proud of my degree and feel that I have the ability to learn any job your organization may give me, and be productive in it.

See there, you have no reason to be defensive about your grades. Instead, turn the question into an opportunity to talk in complimentary terms about yourself.

If your grades are strong, use this to your advantage, by indicating your good work habits, the skills you developed, your ability to compete under pressure, and your ability to be a self-starter. However, don't over-emphasize your schoolwork, lest you be viewed as a "bookworm" or a one-dimensional person. People with high grades are sometimes viewed suspiciously, until they can demonstrate some diversity of talents through reference to out-of-class involvements.

7) "Does it Help me to Have Two Majors?"
Often the liberal arts student will try to get a "double-credential" that he or she believes will have greater marketability in job-hunting. This is not an especially good reason to have two majors fields of study. The better reason is that you like both fields very much and are willing to

sacrifice several electives in other departments in order to have depth of study in the two majors.

In the sciences, a double major (say biology and chemistry) would have relevance to certain fields of work (the food processing business), but the demands of two science majors would deprive the student of many electives and would reduce his or her outside activity time to a minimum. Hence, there is a robbing-from-Peter-to-pay-Paul effect here.

In humanities and social sciences, double majors might apply to certain kinds of work (Spanish and sociology, perhaps, for a person seeking social service work with Central American refugees), but it is possible for other liberal arts graduates to seek these jobs too. And, for most jobs, it matters little what your major was, because any liberal arts graduate can apply. So, having two majors is little different than having one.

If it makes you feel better to have two majors attached to your degree, go ahead and do it. But don't expect employers to jump out of their chairs because of your double-barreled academic program. They are more likely to be interested in your functional skills, your motivation for their field of work, and your ability to communicate well. Transcripts are academic when it comes to the job market. One degree is roughly as good as another. You can "sell" your specific coursework to some extent, but employers are much more concerned about clues to your ability to perform the job they need done.

8) "How do I Sell Myself to an Employer?"

This is the bush we have been beating around for the past few pages. Grades, courses on your transcript, and the reputation of your college are of interest to employers only so far as they suggest how good a worker you are likely to be and your potential for leadership in their organization. Of course, interviewers want to know everything about you—your off-campus experiences, your work history, your campus activities, etc. Your job is to make it easy for interviewers to interpret all this information by disclosing the following factors for them:

a) Skills - The tasks you can perform, as a result of the skills you have developed during the past four or five years, Such as: writing, researching, negotiating, keeping track of money, organizing people and supervising, etc.

b) Motivation - How your interests and experiences have led you to apply for this field. "What makes you really want this job?" is a question on the mind of any good interviewer.

c) Personality - What kind of person are you? Will you be agreeable to work with, and will you fit into the organization? You reveal this not so much by design, as simply by being yourself, being open and responsive to the people you meet during job interviews.

41

"Selling yourself" thus works this way—you get a clear picture of the requirements of the job you are seeking, and then tell an interviewer:

"Selling yourself" thus works this way—you get a clear picture of the requirements of the job you are seeking, and then tell an interviewer:

a) "I know that I can do this job because of these skills that I have developed in my previous experiences, namely _____."

b) "I know that I want this job. It interests me greatly because_____, and I hope to grow into a leadership role in this organization, because _____."

If you can answer "Why do you want this job?" and "Why do you believe we should hire you?" with conviction, and back them up with data and experiences from your background, you will have done a fine job of "selling yourself" to any prospective employer.

My Favorite "Irrelevant" College Courses

The next great breakthrough will occur when liberal arts graduates recognize that the processes of learning are more highly valued than the content that they learned in college. As an employer, I don't care what you know about the Crimean War, but I do care that you can relate disconnected events, that you can do research, and that you have historical vision.

Most liberal arts graduates pursue careers in fields of work that are largely unrelated to their undergraduate majors. They prosper and are happy in their work, yet they did not have "vocational training." How is this so? They applied learning processes to their new jobs in order to handle content that they had not seen before.

I suspect the liberal arts courses which did me the most good were those farthest removed from the pragmatic world, from "vocational training." I wish that I had paid more attention to them. These "irrelevant courses" tested my mind and opened me up to new vistas of thinking. Ultimately they have had a great impact on my career potential. The following courses now seem the most "educational" of all to me. To the extent that I gave them my attention, my career has prospered:

Philosophy - taught me to reason carefully, to probe questions to discover the underlying issues, to think on a large scale.

Languages - encouraged me to understand various people who are "different," appreciate their attitudes about life, and do my best to communicate with them.

Poetry - introduced me to the magic of thinking in visual images, sensitized me to the beauty and rhythm of language, helped me to see that less is more and more is less.

Religion - encouraged me to understand "spirituality" in its

"The great truths are too important to be new."

Novelist Somerset Maugham

"It is essential that the student acquire an understanding of and a lively feeling for values. He must acquire a vivid sense of the beautiful and of the morally good. Otherwise he—with his specialized knowledge —more closely resembles a well-trained dog than a harmoniously developed person."

Albert Einstein
Physicist

widest and deepest sense, and why it is vital to every life and career choice

English - allowed me to experience great writers and thinkers, to be humbled by the dullness of my own prose, and to aspire to grasp "big ideas."

Music - helped me to discover the artist in me and in others, without even learning to play an instrument; helped me to see that materialism has an opposite, a worthy competitor

Science - taught me to appreciate the genius and the rigors of hypothesis testing as it applies to every life decision; exposed me to the mysteries of life as well as to know phenomena.

Mathematics - taught me to see the mathematics which underlies many human ideas and events, the calculus of possibilities, and the pervasiveness of probabilities in everyday life.

Every liberal arts graduate has his or her own list of favorite courses, the importance of which emerge only after years of reflection. I encourage every student to value these courses and recognize that they are a higher level of "career preparation." The student who has the freedom and confidence to take courses which challenge his or her mind, and can set aside the narrow-minded anxiety of "what will these courses do for my career?" is the student who will respond well to unexpected challenges and new problems at work. A flexible, versatile, and far-ranging mind is the best defense against career obsolescence, the best set of tools to have when jobs and careers turn inside-out, as they inevitably do in the course of one's working lifetime.

"My curriculum in college included too many science courses for premedical students which were taught over again in medical school. This didn't permit important courses in English, speech, business, art, and the humanities which are important in insuring a fruitful and rich life."

San Jose State
University graduate

I Tell Them I'm A Liberal Arts Major

And then, of course, they say: how quaint; and what are you
going to do with that?
What am I going to do with it?
As though these four phenomenal years were an object I could
cart away from college—
a bachelor's degree across my back like an ermine jacket,
or my education hung from a ceiling on a string.
What am I going to do with it?
Well, I thought perhaps I'd put it in a cage
to see if it multiplies or does tricks or something
so I could enter it in a circus
and realize a sound dollar-for-dollar return
on my investment.
Then, too, I am exploring the possibility of
whipping it out like a folding chair
at V.F.W. parades and Kiwanis picnics.
I might have it shipped and drive it through Italy.
Or sand it down and sail it.
What am I going to do with it?
I'll tell you one thing:
I'm probably never going to plant sod around it.
You see, I'm making it a definitive work:
repapering parts of my soul
that can never be toured by my friends;
wine glass balanced in one hand,
warning guests to watch the beam
that hits people on the head
when they go downstairs to see the den.
You don't understand—
I'm using every breath to tread water
in all-night swimming competitions
with Hegel, Marx, and Wittgenstein;
I am a reckless diver fondling the bottom of civilization
for ropes of pearls;
I am whispering late into the night on a river bank with Zola;
I am stopping often, soaking wet and exhausted, to weep
at the Bastille.
What am I going to do with it?

I'm going to sneak it away from my family
gathered for my commencement
and roam the high desert
making love to it.

Carol Jin Evans
Metropolitan State College

The Normal Problems of Liberal Arts Job Hunters

Problem Numero Uno

My major field in college was not the
field of work I wanted to enter.
(Perhaps you want to be a financial
analyst but majored in Slavic languages.)

This is the essential problem of all liberal arts graduates. It is easily licked via a three part plan for use during college or by using another three steps after graduation.

DURING COLLEGE

"Average managers are concerned with methods, opinions, precedents. Good managers are concerned with solving problems."

*Management expert
A. Marshall Jones*

During college, your three part plan might look like this.

(1) Get Experience -
Whatever occupation you intend to enter, find some paid or unpaid experience in that area of work. It can be a part-time job, summer job, internship, volunteer experience, or anything else. "Experience" communicates that you are motivated toward this field, that you have had exposure to the daily realities of that field, and that you are willing to work for what you want.

(2) Take Enough Courses To Show You Are Serious -
Take a few courses related to the field you want to enter. It is OK for liberal art students to take business courses, or journalism courses, or advertising courses, etc. A little background knowledge may help you, and will communicate to an employer that you care enough about the field to study it.

(3) Develop Skills -
Find out what skills are important in your intended field and cultivate these skills in whatever way you can. In the example above, a financial analyst would need quantitative skills, analytical skills, data collection skills, and probably writing skills. Look at your coursework, out-of-class activities, and work experience to see which of these skills you already possess. For those you are missing, you must latch onto new experiences that will nurture new skills.

After graduating, whether or not you were able to use the three steps during college, there is still plenty of hope for you. Three tactics have been found helpful.

(1) Go For It -

Completely bereft of experience, courses, or skills, you may think it foolish to apply for the job you want. Maybe not. If you have a strong feeling that a field is right for you, and you believe you can learn it if you're just given the chance, then the old saying "Nothing ventured, nothing gained" comes into play. Enthusiasm and tactful assertiveness can do wonders for the new liberal arts graduate. Employers like spunk, straightforwardness, and they like knowing you are interested in them. If this doesn't work right away, try the next two points in the plan.

(2) Interim Job -

To keep body and soul together while you're looking for the real thing, take a different job that may not fit your plans at all. Take the job for any of these reasons: it is convenient - it enables you to earn decent money - it is enjoyable - it gives you some kind of bridge to the job you really want - it gives you access to people you want to meet. An interim job might be a junior version of the job you covet, perhaps a low-level grunt job at an organization where you really want to be. Maybe that's the way a lot of people start in that field.

Interim jobs sometimes turn out better than you think. You may unconsciously choose an area that taps into some of your hidden needs. Even if this is not true, the interim job gives you valuable time to keep up your search without going into debt, depression, or despair.

"Most of the fields I have worked in are not covered by specific college courses."

Colorado State University graduate

(3) Get Experience -

Sound familiar? Yes, experience is The Great Equalizer in job-hunting. Get it wherever or however you can, so interviewers cannot accuse you of being a complete greenhorn or dilettante. You have several options - post-graduate internships, part-time experience, volunteer work, apprenticeships. Failing all of that, you can show how you have developed "transferrable skills" from previous jobs or responsibilities. Career counselors (see "Sources of Help" in a later section of this chapter) can assist you in identifying these skills and relating them to what your target employer needs.

EXAMPLE: Here is how Joe Freebush, the history major who wants to become a financial analyst pieced together his During College and After Graduation three part strategies.

Joe Freebush
History Major
Job Objective: Financial Analyst

During college...

Experiences: Worked as a research assistant in a stock brokerage house. Volunteered to help a faculty member with a journal article for a financial publication by collecting investment reports and plotting recommendations.

Courses: "Money and Banking" (Business School)
"Securities and Investments" (Business School)
"Advanced Statistics" (Psychology Department)

Skills: Worked in trust department of local bank for a summer becoming familiar with financial transactions, investment strategies, and resources used by those in the field.

After college...

Interim jobs: Research assistant for a real estate developer. Statistical data analyst for an airline.

Experience: Volunteered to work ten hours a week as an unpaid assistant to a financial analyst in a highly-regarded brokerage house.

Prior to the interim job, negotiated a half-time, low-pay internship with the investment department of a state bank.

"Whatever may be our natural talents, the art of writing is not acquired all at once."

Jean Jacques Rousseau
Philosopher

Problem Numero Two

Disillusionment

Business graduates, and other professional students are usually fired up about their job targets and have been pointing toward them for a long time. Liberal arts graduates, on the other hand, have mixed feelings about the whole thing, feelings that may include apprehension, vague uncertainty, or active disdain. In many ways, liberal arts graduates enter the job search as reluctant dragons, having the ability to slay those employers, but not entirely sure if they want to.

This disillusionment usually takes the form of these two questions.

(1) "What is There to do That's Interesting?"

This is the natural result of years with Plato, Hegel, Hemingway, Van Gogh, Beethoven, Freud, Shakespeare, Rousseau, and other friends of the liberal arts student. Four or more years with the great thinkers, the sweep of history, and the broader perspectives on life can make a "job" seem awfully dull.

Some liberal arts graduates are ready to get to work, but others feel limited and almost saddened by the pragmatism and sharply focused problems of the profit and non-profit worlds. This is not an easy transition. What's a liberal arts person to do? First of all, recognize that entry-level jobs are going to be less thrilling than you would like. Give the job a chance. It leads to better things—promotions, new projects, and greater levels of responsibility. Secondly, look for the jobs that DO have challenge. The same analytical skills you developed in philosophy courses or elsewhere can help you to understand why a business is losing its market share, or why a magazine needs to appeal to a different readership. The same breadth of human understanding that you got from anthropology can help you to plan programs for economically blighted areas where people have varying racial and ancestral backgrounds.

(2) "Why is This Taking so Long?"

Job-hunting does take a little longer for the liberal arts graduate, and this gap between graduation and employment gets a lot of bad press, not to mention gnashing of parents' teeth and sidelong looks from friends with the engineering degrees who happen to have caught the wave and look as if they are on Easy Street. Their high ride can end, because markets change, demand for engineers can shift dramatically, and their earnings tend to top out if and when they cannot qualify for managerial or senior project leader roles.

The liberal arts graduate has a big leap to make—from a focus on broad learning skills to a focus on specific employers —and it can leave you feeling a little cold as the winds of September and October brush your face when you're walking to an interim job or a part-time job that you are hoping will develop into something bigger. You're getting impatient for progress and tired of hearing how your friends are earning more money than you. This is normal stuff. Your disillusionment will fade as you get work experience and demonstrate your ability to learn. Your time is coming. The pages that follow will tell you why. Meanwhile, talk with a few graduates who have been working for a few years. You'll see how they have advanced and this will give you the perspective you need.

"There is a time in the affairs of men, which, taken at the flood, leads on to fortune."

William Shakespeare
Julius Caesar

48

Problem Numero Three
(you may not recognize it as a problem)
Narrowness of many liberal arts programs

"Acquire new knowledge while thinking over the old and you may become a teacher of others."

Chinese philosopher Confucius

We hope that you infer from this book that it is safe to study liberal arts but there is no guarantee that everyone who earns a liberal arts degree will acquire the qualities so highly prized by employers. In fact, many will not. There is just as much danger of students within liberal arts schools taking too narrow a program as there is danger of overspecialization in preprofessional schools.

An English major who takes 18 literature courses, while ignoring mathematics, language, and science will be just as narrow and ill-prepared for career advancement as a finance or electrical engineering major who sidesteps humanities courses and never writes a term paper. The liberal arts graduate has no stranglehold on "liberal skills." These skills are available to anyone who had the inclination to acquire them.

A survey conducted in 1988 with support from the National Endownment from the Humanities highlighted the problem for both liberal arts and other students. The study discovered that it was possible to graduate from 80 percent of the nation's four year colleges and universities without taking a single course in the history of western civilization. In fact in 1988-89 it was possible to earn a bachelor's degree from:

> 37 percent of the nation's colleges and universities without taking any course in history;

> 45 percent without taking a course in American or English literature;

> 62 percent without taking a course in philosophy;

> 77 percent without studying a foreign language. [1]

Unfortunately, too many students arrive on campuses lacking a broad base of knowledge, and lacking contact with many areas of study they too often graduate without many of the courses which help to provide depth in college—and in life.

[1] *"Humanities in America" Chronicle of Higher Education September 21, 1988.*

"The object of poetry is truth, not individual and local, but general and operative; not standing upon external testimony but carried alive into the heart by passion."

William Wordsworth
Author

Liberal learning is an attitude of questioning and mind-stretching that transcends degree labels. It comes from teachers who challenge the mind, courses which examine universal questions, and from the student who views elasticity of thought as more important than information. A bachelor's degree graduate need not come to an employer with"vocational training" on his or her transcript to be welcomed by the employer. But, if the theme is liberal education then the college transcript should show diversity and a broadbased program of general education.

CAREER PROFILE

"Having communications skills is going to be a very, very big plus. Banks today have to become more people-oriented, because of so much competition."

David Hensley

BA, Sociology/Anthropology 1978
Now, Vice-President (Lending)
Frontier National Bank

Liberal Arts Education

In liberal arts, you have a chance to view more courses, you have more things available to you; it helps give you a larger outlook on life. Through liberal arts, I developed writing and speaking skills, and the ability to communicate with people on more than one level. Because banking is still very much a people business, the ability to communicate with others on a one-to-one basis is one of the most important skills you can possess, so my education in that direction has been invaluable to me.

Job Search Techniques/Results

Before joining Frontier National Bank I held positions in retail, engineering, and advertising sales. The sales job was with a radio station, and it was through contacts made there that I got to know some of Frontier National's organizers and was given a chance to be a business development person. I was lucky to have a president who was interested in my career, and willing to let me prove myself. I started some banking courses, and began training for a loan officer's position while still in marketing and business development.

I was appointed Assistant Vice President: Loan Officer. I handled loans for individuals and light commercial customers, prepared reports for the Board on the bank's loan performance, and handled advertising. My present title is Vice President - Commercial Lending. Although I still maintain consumer loan customers, my primary responsibilities include new commercial loan requests and loan workouts. I also prepare board reports on the bank's loan performance and handle the bank's advertising.

Job Advice

First, don't be afraid of your degree choice. Enjoy it. Enjoy what you've learned from it and the exposure you've gotten from all the various areas you've covered. I guarantee you that you will have covered much more and been exposed to much more through a liberal arts education than many people will be in their lives.

Job Advice—I think there's a certain amount of latitude that every person is given to try new things. If you don't know exactly what you want to do, as I didn't, don't be afraid to experiment in various career paths, to gain overall experience. Coming out of college, you're still fairly young, and that's the best time to try new things. Working through college helps, not only to give you experience, but also in helping you to have a realistic perspective on what's out there. College is an insulated environment, and working makes you realize that there's more coming up in the world and that you have to prepare yourself.

I believe that you need to be involved in the world around you. Rising through a company, being good at what you do, requires setting your goals a little higher than usual and having the self-esteem and guts to go out there and keep trying. If you set your goals and work hard enough, you can obtain them pretty rapidly.

Also, if you can, find a support system. It always helps to have someone there praising you and patting you on the back. As far as getting into some type of banking, I think liberal arts majors should take some basic accounting courses, computer programming, writing skills, even speech classes. Many large banks are requiring finance/accounting degrees or, MBA's. Liberal arts is an excellent degree path for MBA work. Smaller banks will, however, still accept other degree plans.

Having communication skills is going to be a very, very big plus. Banks today have to become more people-oriented, because of so much competition. Remember, too, that you've already displayed the ability to graduate from college, to make decent grades and to think on your feet. When you go into the interview, you've got to impress the people with the way you present yourself and with your general business philosophy. Don't be afraid to use your overall knowledge—they're looking for people who can think. You're going to have on-the-job training anyway—any business worth its salt will invest in training you to a certain area.

Be prepared to work hard, and even though you may start out at a lower salary than someone in a specialized area, it doesn't mean you won't rise twice as fast.

Section 8
Helping Liberal Arts Students:
Suggestions for Counselors and Students Themselves

"Those of us who are black and those of us who are women are not encouraged to put our experiences on record. Mankind is a good twenty generations away from being genuinely tolerant, yet what distinguishes human beings from other mammals is their ability to both project and reflect. We do these things through books, by means of people writing about the things that are happening in their lives."

Nikki Giovanni
(Career Insights, 1984)

This text and the references and studies cited in Section 12 tells us "Liberal Arts is OK." But, teachers and counselors must be aware that many liberal learners have a problem

When put on the defensive by employment interviewers, too many of today's liberal arts graduates have trouble with the question, "Why did you study liberal arts?" Since experience shows that faculty are often slow to jump in and articulate answers, much of the burden for helping students think this through falls on counselors and career placement officers. We cannot expect graduates of liberal education, exposed to today's media and conflicting opinions on the college campus, to move into employment interviews with automatic confidence. Most need some help.

Though it might be tempting to pit liberal versus specialized college education and tally the results as shown by alumni, I do not see this a a rivalry which must be settled. The more important question is "What is the nature of the relationship between liberal learning and career development?" In this overreaching question we have several unanswered questions and a strong need among students, parents. graduates, and faculty to answer them. I hope that future studies, analyses, and articles will be directed toward these major concerns.

What remains to be done?

(1) First, like the ghost of Christmas past, students continue to raise that key question, "What can I do with my major?"

It is limiting and frustrating for a student to approach liberal education as if the major is their "vocational preparation," yet they persist in so doing and their parents and others often encourage this line of thought. We must strive to expand the vision of liberal arts students to help them to see that their total educational experience is what matters the most. With strong general learning skills they are better prepared for work - and for life. Too many students continue to look upon their major as their career preparation and are frustrated by a narrow question with little chance of successful answers.

(2) Career counselors must communicate the career prospects for their students to liberal arts faculty members.

Faculty members must communicate with students about the meaning of liberal education and they will do this more effectively, and be encouraged to do so, by having more information on the careers of past graduates. Too many students pick up misunderstandings about the marketability of a liberal arts degree long before they ever meet their career counselor and, thus, that counseling starts with at least one strike against it. Some feel that teachers may convey the impression that liberal arts is hard to sell in the marketplace because they themselves wonder what they would ever do if they left academe.

(3) A liberal education is important for ALL college students.

We must communicate to all departments in our colleges and universities that the skills and attributes nurtured by a broadbased liberal education program are valued highly by employers. Specialized graduates should take some liberal arts courses because their lack of them may later handicap their development into organizational managers or leaders. Infusing liberal learning into specialized college curricula is not a popular topic among faculty of either liberal arts or specialized programs.

That is exactly why we emphasize the point here. Fortunately, we are not the only voices in the wilderness. In 1987, the prestigious Massachusetts Institute of Technology announced curriculum changes designed to give engineers more classroom time in general education courses.

(4) How does liberal learning relate to career advancement?

We have the beginnings of the answer to that question but more insight is needed. Additional studies are required to help us understand the qualities which liberal education encourages and how these qualities are useful in meeting the practical problems of the world. How important, for example, is inter-disciplinary learning? How helpful have been the specialized courses which some liberal arts students have worked into their programs? Is writing an important skill in all careers? Is it desirable to put off taking specialized college courses until one is fairly certain about long-range career goals? These and many other questions need to be investigated.

(5) How much can we predict the nature of future demand for college graduates?

I suspect the labor market is always shifting and unpredictable. (If you doubt this, consider how demand for geologists and petroleum engineers languished in the 1960's, rose to a fever pitch in the 1970s, and dropped down again in the 1980s.) We need to communicate that employment demand is uncertain and varies so that college students will better understand that they can't build college programs to keep pace with yesterday's, or even today's, demand. Fifteen years ago, Ivar Berg told us in **Education and Jobs: The Great Training Robbery** that college programs can't be matched to job market trends and that is still true today and will likely be true tomorrow.

(6) How many different careers might a college graduate conceivably enter?

We have not fully explored Donald Super's original principle of Multi-Potentiality which states that everyone (particularly an able college graduate) is capable of pursuing successfully many different kinds of work. Is it true? I strongly suspect that it is.

(7) What are the qualities that most characterize people who are successful in their work?

I would hypothesize that the attributes of success are very similar from one field of work or profession to another. Klemp found this to be true but many other studies are needed to learn the qualities most universally related to success. The more evidence we uncover of generic "success" qualities the less students may need to rely on credentials/specialized degree programs as union cards/qualifications for entry to occupations.

(8) It would be helpful to reaffirm for those who live and love the liberal arts that career counselors are not trying to vocationalize or otherwise undermine liberal learning.

Through informal meetings, coauthorship of articles, and in many other ways, bridges may be built between those specializing in career counseling and those teaching in liberal arts fields. Liberal learnings for careers and liberal learning for life are not antagonists. They are compatible. Career counselors and faculty members need to meet together and agree on this.

Should Liberal Arts be Combined with Specialized Courses?

I mentioned this earlier but as it comes up again and again some final thoughts seem in order. It is tempting to recommend, as many have done, that liberal arts students take some "vocational courses" as an ideal combination of general and specialized learning. However, I think this is an overrated approach to career preparation.

It seems much more important that students have the freedom to plan unique academic programs that suit their needs and preferences. There are many liberal arts graduates who enter jobs and advance well in their careers without any formal coursework related to their occupation. Their clear success clouds the question of what is the best preparation for a certain field of work. Students can take career-specific courses if they choose, and we think it is often helpful, but they should not feel compelled to do so. As pointed out before, "career preparation" can also come from independent study, part-time and summer work, internships, volunteer assignments, research projects, and even college extra-curricula activities. Within certain liberal arts courses (English, economics, psychology, etc.) it may be possible to do a term

"Don't assume that when you choose a major you are choosing a career as well. There is virtually no connection between academic majors in the liberal arts and future career paths."

University of Virginia graduate

55

paper or other project on an area of career interest to a student.

The "combination" approach to career planning may reflect a supermarket mentality that says you can prepare for a career by shopping for the right basket full of knowledge. Liberal skills, interpersonal qualities, perspective, and attitudes toward learning are not given enough attention. In searching for the right combination of course titles, students overlook the attributes that relate most to career advancement. John Munschauer, a prominent author (**Jobs for English Majors and Other Smart People**) who has counseled liberal arts students for many years at Cornell University says:

> There is no college course in judgement. Nor are there any in imagination, shrewdness, leadership, reflectiveness, wittiness, integrity, intelligence, or any of the basic traits that relate to job performance.

Let's face it. College is the best opportunity (some say the last good opportunity) where a person has the time and resources to learn that democracy and capitalism were not here when God created heaven and earth, that the railroads did not die from tuberculosis, and that the economic interests of America are intimately intertwined with the cultures and religious philosophies of Third World countries. It is the best time for them to find out that their own "bottom lines" (or, preferred life styles) are being affected by the people in other cultures whose motives they do not understand.

College is the one time individuals learn that their careers are part of the larger drama of diverse people trying to live peacefully and productively under one global roof. I would prefer not to deprive them of these kinds of learning, because they may want these insights many years later when it is to late to find the classes and teachers who can provide them.

What Kinds of Work Can Liberal Arts Graduates Do?

"New Hope for Liberal Arts"

How many times have you seen that headline? It appears optimistic, but look again. "New hope" implies that up until that moment, things were pretty gloomy. Or maybe, the patient has just been revived from cardiac arrest. It implies that perhaps liberal arts may live to see another day. Well, if that's what it means, I protest. Liberal arts has never been out of favor. Its graduates have consistently been employed at all levels of industry, in all sectors of the labor market, and in all kinds of economic conditions. Liberal arts graduates continue to rise to positions of leadership, even in the face of the emerging array of business degrees and other vocationally oriented programs at the bachelor's level.

If liberal arts has any problem at all, it is modesty in its public relations. People too often forget that they have liberal arts graduates working beside them, above them, next door, and all around. Some liberal arts graduates in the 1960s and 1970s didn't get hired immediately upon graduation and a lot of folks panicked unnecessarily. In truth, a lot of engineers and other specialists had some troubles in those days also. The "resurgence" of liberal arts is not a comeback at all, but simply a reminder that liberal arts alumni have been there all along - in the boardrooms, managerial positions, and in other roles of influence.

Can the liberal arts graduate do "just about anything?" Is that an exaggeration cooked up by the newly rejuvenated public relations department of liberal education? No, it is not just hype, but a simple statement of the candy-store variety of options open to a liberal arts job seeker. How is this possible? Consider any job that liberal arts graduates might want. These three avenues are open to them:

1) Acquire experience and/or skills during undergraduate school which will help you to compete for the job at graduation.

(2) Get hired and learn that position through on-the-job experience. In some cases, this may involve working in a related position preparing for the job you really want.

(3) Complete a graduate degree that would qualify you for the job. You may be taking these advanced courses along with your fellow students who had majored in business or other specialized fields.

"Who will society turn to in the next century to ponder the impact of technological change on the human condition? Computer scientists? Who will we rely on to explain this change to the average citizen. Engineers? Obviously not. Only those people with a solid foundation in the humanities will be able to cope with the changes which we will see in the upcoming decades."

Harry Campbell,
President,
Wadsworth Publishers of Canada,
Ltd.

Of course, these three strategies will not work for ALL jobs in the labor market. Specialists are going to be required to design nuclear power plants, install accounting systems, and solve complex aerodynamic problems. But such specialization is required for only a small proportion of the jobs open to college graduates and these are not the kinds of positions which interest most liberal art graduates, anyway.

The variety of options open to liberal arts graduates highlights careers open to those without advanced degrees, which is how the majority of liberal arts graduates arrive on the job market.

There are many excellent books listed in Section II which describe major job categories open to liberal arts graduates. See **Wanted: Liberal Arts Graduates, Liberal Arts Jobs, Life After Shakespeare, High Tech Jobs for Non-Tech Grads and The High Tech Career Guide.**

Wanted: Liberal Arts Graduates by Salzman and Better cites numerous fields in the business world that are rich in opportunities for liberal art graduates:

Accounting

"Forget the green eye-shade and the mechanical pencil tucked behind your ear... The old stereotype of the boring number-cruncher no longer holds true...A career in accounting requires strong mathematical skills as well as the ability to analyze data, communicate effectively, and work well with others...There are two fields of accounting open to liberal arts graduates: management accounting and public accounting...In general, liberal arts graduates enter management accounting with one of several titles; internal auditor, cost accountant, plant accountant, and data processor are common...Most liberal arts graduates enter public accounting firms as accounting trainees, becoming junior or staff accountants after completing training."

Advertising

"Advertising is the happy home of many liberal arts graduates...most liberal arts graduates enter the advertising industry as junior account executives or copywriters, market researchers, media assistants, production assistants, or sales representatives. Since advertising is a high turnover field, entry-level jobs open frequently. However, competition is extremely stiff."

Consulting

"Consulting is perhaps the most competitive field for freshly minted BA's to enter...Generally speaking, consulting firms seek the very best and brightest graduates. They look for new hires who are highly articulate, objective, self-confident, and resilient...Liberal arts graduates generally enter the consulting business as research associates or assistants...since the vertical structure of most consulting firms is quite lean,

Seventy percent of a group of Lehigh University alumni who majored in English would do it again.

College English
(January 1985)

"It is a fantastic advantage to be able to carry on a conversation on almost any topic with almost any person. In my career, personal contact is vitally important."

Commodities Broker,
University of Texas graduate

research associates can move up rapidly. After two to three years, you can become a senior associate or a consultant."

Finance
"Commercial banks are among the best employers of liberal arts graduates. Each year dozens of recruiters scour the nation's campuses in search of talented students eager to enter the field...Most banks start recent graduates as trainees, after which they become loan officers...

"The investment bank has many different specialty areas. The corporate (or public) finance department issues stocks and bonds; the brokerage department buys and sells these instruments, and the trading department matches buyers and sellers to earn money on fluctuations in the marketplace...Competition for entry-level jobs or training spots within the top investment banks is tough...After two years as an analyst, many liberal arts graduates go on to business school and then return as associates.

"Liberal arts graduates usually enter insurance companies as actuaries, claim representatives, underwriters, agents, or brokers. While no specific degree is best for a career in insurance, you should have good quantitative, analytical, and rational abilities. Course work in statistics and mathematics is a help."

Human Resources
"As corporations increasingly recognize the importance of organizational efficiency and effectiveness, human resources play a vital role in American business...Once known as personnel, the human resources function exists in all areas of private and public industry, as well as in government and education...Entry-level jobs for liberal arts graduates...as generally found in three departments: training and development, labor relations and recruiting, and placement."

Manufacturing
"Liberal arts graduates interested in a career in industrial management generally take one of the following paths: production, inventory control, purchasing, or merchandising...While manufacturing jobs currently don't have a place in the limelight, they shouldn't be discounted. Often they're the best pathway up an organization, since on a day-to-day basis they involve the "real thing" - producing products...It allows a recent graduate to make a very real impact on a company's bottom line."

Marketing and Sales
"Marketing involves finding new products and services and improving existing ones, while sales involves finding customers who will buy these goods. Both areas are excellent employers of liberal arts graduates...Imagination, intuition, and initiative play a big role in marketing, which deals with

"Whatever you accomplish, someone helps you."

Althea Gibson,
World Champion Tennis Player

consumer research and product/service evaluation. Liberal arts graduates usually enter this area as marketing assistants, working with brand managers to learn how consumer needs can be met better, faster, cheaper...Sales representatives must be self-starters and they must be able to face rejection. Most large companies train liberal arts graduates for several months and then put them out in the field to sell."

Public Relations

"Currently more than 150,000 people are employed in the industry, working as writers, editors, researchers, speakers, producers, and managers...You'll be expected to have excellent writing and speaking skills, and to be creative with ideas and language...most new hires learn by working on press releases, speech writing, employee publications, company newsletters, shareholders reports, and other internal/external communications."

Life After Shakespeare by Flores-Esteves details other interesting and promising fields that liberal arts graduates can enter. Here are some fields of work which may not be widely known to liberal arts graduates:

Cultural Organizations

"Cultural work includes jobs with museums, art organizations, ethnic organizations, information centers, art galleries, civic centers, historic places, government agencies, community centers, convention centers, intercultural organizations, and other nonprofit organizations...Museums employ a large diversified staff...most museum employees have a B.A. or less. Heads of departments often have higher degrees."

Environmental Protection

"Occupations in the fields of conservation, environmental protection, and ecology cover water treatment, irrigation, noise control, air pollution, land, fish, and wildlife management,...solid waste management, radiation control, research and development, and design. Other interesting jobs in this field include environmental lobbyist, rural sociologist, population analyst, and range-animal nutritionist...Some of the employers that hire people are consultants, state and federal agencies, private industry, colleges and universities, citizens' groups, trade associations, research laboratories, and scientific associations."

"I have only one life, and it is short enough. Why waste it on things I don't want most."

Supreme Court Justice Louis Brandeis

"The direction in which education starts a man will determine his future life."

Plato,
The Republic

Foreign Affairs Organizations
Working in the United States:

"Consider working with organizations dealing with foreign assistance or foreign relations that are based in the United States. Examples include The Asia Foundation, The Council on Foreign Relations, World Neighbor, The Experiment in International Living, and The Overseas Development Council."

Foundations

"Foundations are endowed institutions that...are established to maintain or aid social, educational, scientific, and humanistic activities serving the common welfare, primarily through the awarding of grants...Entry-level positions with foundations include those of aides, researchers, and proposal reviewers. In addition, some foundations have internship or programs to train future professionals."

Government

"Government employment is a favorite job-prospecting ground that offers many advantages for generalists and liberal arts graduates...job security, direct contact with the public, good salaries at the professional level, positions that are not overpopulated with advanced degree-holders, good advancement opportunities, and transferrable skills. Most important, you are doing public service work. There are four civil service systems available to you: federal, state, county, and city."

International Service: Working in Foreign Nations

"Probably the best-known international service agency is the Foreign Service of the State Department...Others...include the United States Information Agency, Agency for International Development, Peace Corps, and Department of Defense...Teaching abroad is another possibility. It ranges from teaching with U.S. agencies...to teaching English as a foreign language for foreign governments and teaching in schools operated by private American companies."

Lobbying

"Many public and private sector lobbyists start by becoming thoroughly familiar with issues relating to a specific area. They become 'experts' on the environment, the arts, students' concerns, rent control, or a specific product. Others start by working directly with the staff of a lobbyist...doing research, preparing articles, news releases, and similar materials for dissemination to the press and the public."

Public Affairs Organizations

"Volunteer and aide positions, as well as internships, are good ways to enter the public affairs field. Examples of public affairs organizations include Amnesty International, National

Urban League, American Civil Liberties Union, Constitutional Rights Foundation, League of Women Voters, and the Council On Economic Priorities."

Publishing

"Publishing is a huge business in the United States. It includes books, magazines, newspapers, and other periodicals, such as journals devoted to specific fields. Book publishing alone produces thousands of new titles every year. It employs people...as editors, writers, publicists, illustrators, advertising workers, printers, and mechanics."

Recreation and Leisure

"People in recreation services provide leadership in...parks, playgrounds, camps, and community centers...People who work in the field of recreation resources find employment in...botanical gardens, parks, monuments, historical sites, zoos, aquariums, information centers, and beaches...Commercial amusement and entertainment enterprises provide work in amusement parks, stadiums, gold clubs, ski resorts, sports arenas, convention centers, tennis clubs, private camps, boating resorts, sports clubs, health spas, retirement homes, recreation travel agencies, etc,"

Research

"Entry-level positions include research technician, research aide, statistician, and trainee. They...collect and analyze information on specified subjects, make judgements through observation and interviews...construct and test methods of data collection,...write reports and interpret findings. Sample organizations include The Hudson Institute, the National Bureau of Economic Research, The Brookings Institution, The Institute of Social Research, Market Opinion Research, and the Center for Applied Linguistics."

"After 10 years I just realized what I really learned at U.Va., unbeknownst to me while it was happening - i.e. how to think and solve problems. This is the single most important factor in my current success."

University of Virginia English major.

Social Service

" There is a myth about social work; many people see it in terms of welfare and food stamps...(however) there is a great diversity of functions and areas of employment; abortion reform, adoption services, drug abuse, employment, family life, minority groups, battered women, child abuse, family planing,...help lines, the disabled, immigration services, gay advocacy, housing, population, safety, sex information, suicide prevention, youth services, and women's rights, among others."

Writing

"Some writing occupations are columnist, copywriter, critic, editorial writer, humorist, librettist, lyricist, playwright, screen writer, and newscaster...Other jobs for writers are found in advertising, arts reviewing, associations, audio-visual writing, business writing, commercial reports, genealogy and local history, government public information, radio continuity, speech writing, and technical writing."

CAREER PROFILE

"My ability to absorb a broad spectrum of knowledge has been most helpful, and it's not something I would have acquired in a narrower discipline."

Cherie Wentworth

BA, Economics, 1968
Account Representative
Xerox Corporation

Liberal Arts Education

Following a liberal arts curriculum helped me learn how to study and how to learn a lot of different things. Language courses and courses involving writing helped me most.

The language experience gave me the skills to learn electronics and computer languages—technical jargon.

Also, I did a lot of writing as a liberal arts student, and I find that clear, concise writing skills are necessary now, because I write out lengthy proposals involving complicated information, and I must make that information understandable to the customer.

Creative thinking, creative problem solving, and a general knowledge of how the world works are important qualities—all of which are developed in a liberal arts program. My ability to absorb a broad spectrum of knowledge has been most helpful, and it's not something I would have acquired in a narrower discipline. I would have learned one thing, and that's not what you need in the business world.

Job Search Techniques/Results

I worked with Bell Telephone prior to Xerox; in a roundabout way, it was through that job that I came here. The Xerox machine in the office at Bell Telephone was broken, so I took it apart and started to fix it. The Xerox technician told me that if I was able to fix that machine, I should go to work for them—an idea that would never have occurred to me on my own. But with his impetus, I applied at Xerox, passed their test and went through training.

I started with Xerox in 1976, and worked very successfully as a technician for two and one half years. Then they moved me into management, a position I was qualified for because of my liberal arts degree, some previous work experience as a supervisor, and because I demonstrated a willingness to develop myself by spending five months working on management training on my own time. I was in management for five years, and then they offered me a position in sales, which is where I am now.

The responsibilities involved in this position are quite complicated. I have certain accounts, called vertical markets, with which I work. I deal with some real estate companies and all of the the commercial printers in town.

Making a sale can be a long process. It usually takes several months for me to get to know all the decision makers, meet the people using office equipment and acquaint them with how to use it, and to judge whether or not our equipment fits their needs.

After several months, I meet with the ultimate decision makers. We sit down with a written proposal, and I go over it with them. I have to be very clear about what their business does. I also have to be familiar with all the equipment, its functions, price plans, etc. I have to know how to deal with companies, know the Xerox rental plan, the Xerox financial purchase plans, how banks work, the administrative procedure, etc. I have to understand billings and make sure that the customer is serviced correctly after the sale. It's basically a complicated job that involves an understanding of broad aspects of the business world as well as specific information about a piece of equipment.

Job Advice

Going into the interview, be prepared. Know the company and the position you want—not necessarily the title—but be able to describe clearly the type of job you want. Look up the company; read periodicals and annual reports. Know the direction of the company—their future outlook, what's important to them, etc.

Find out as much as you can, so that you'll be able to ask intelligent questions. It's very important in an interview to be able to ask questions. You need to show the interviewer that you have knowledge about the company and that you know yourself.

Sales is something that I never thought of, but it's an excellent position for liberal arts students, and a liberal arts background can be sold to an employer very easily.

Remember that most companies provide training. Xerox provides excellent sales training, but you have to be willing to do a lot on your own time as well.

Above all, don't limit yourself, and don't let people limit you. Look at your skills, no matter what they are, and try to see how they could apply to different types of jobs. I've done everything from climbing telephone poles to managing technicians at Xerox to selling high tech products, and in all cases, my liberal arts background has been a benefit.

People Who Can Help Liberal Arts Students with Their Careers

Who's Here to Help?

Flexibility, breadth of knowledge, and leadership potential are inherent in all liberal arts graduates, however, this is no automatic guarantee that you will be able to use these qualities in a worthwhile career, simply by completing your college degree. Well-educated graduates still need bridges to the labor market. Fortunately, these days there are numerous sources of help for college seniors and alumni. It makes little sense to go it alone when you can augment your own efforts with a variety of other resources, many of them highly specialized and experienced with helping people just like you.

As you review sources which may help you, keep in mind these three guidelines:

"College didn't fit me for any certain career but it taught me how to learn."

California State University at Fresno graduate

(1) Don't depend on any single resource but use as many as you can.

(2) If you use three or more of these sources well, you are likely to have a block of job opportunities coming your way.

(3) Don't spend money to get outside help, until you have first gotten maximum help from the free services. Just because an organization charges money for its assistance doesn't mean it offers a better service.

These are some of the sources that may help you. But you can probably augment these with a good list of your own.

(1) College Career Planning and Placement Services.

These offices are found in most of today's colleges and universities. On some larger campuses there are separate organizations for career information and counseling and for job placement services. Whatever system exists on your campus take full advantage of it. Get to know the people in the office who are most likely to offer the help and leads that you need and make sure those people know as much about you as possible.

Most career planning offices have an occupational information library, employer literature rack, books describing specific careers, directories of potential employers in various fields, as well as catalogs and other information about opportunities for further training. Career offices often conduct workshops designed to communicate the job outlook, help candidates brush up on job search skills, or help candidates share information on their job campaigns with each other. Some have computer programs available to help with career planning, such as DISCOVER, SIGI, and CHOICES. Whatever resources may be available make full use of them, the career planning office should become as important in your last days of college as the school library.

(2) On-Campus Recruiting Programs.

At many schools, a number of employing organizations conduct initial interviews in the college career center. These offer one of the easiest ways to make a personal contact with organizations of choice.

The kinds of employers visiting college campuses, however, do not represent an accurate cross-section of organizations which do hiring. Those who come to the colleges to recruit are more likely than others to be seeking engineers, accountants, and other specialized graduates. Often these are those which are generally in short supply all over the country so recruitment is deemed important. But, don't get discouraged if relatively few ask for liberal arts graduates.

The great Invisible Job Market—representing 90% of the jobs available for all college graduates—is wide open for liberal arts graduates. This far broader market includes many large and small companies, government agencies, non-profit organizations, and other employers. These employers do not recruit on campuses because they do not have to. You must contact them yourself—in person, or by telephone and letter.

But, if employers do visit your school, look for those with companies which interest you. Look for those offering jobs for nonspecialists and take advantage of the available interview options. Fortunately, unlike some students who assume that campus interviews are the only job search method, you know that they are but one of the many.

(3) Internships

The work/learning experience goes back quite a few hundred years to the days when Medieval artisans took apprentices under their wings. Today, practical, on-the-job learning may be called an "internship." These may be either paid or unpaid (volunteer) positions. But the key is to locate an organization with a good reputation and a willingness to give you the opportunity to learn while spending enough time with you to make sure that your work is progressing and your duties wide enough to offer a rich learning experience.

Internships offer practical experience and may provide just the key to making employers want to hire you for competitive jobs. Employers, by the way, like the eagerness which interns often bring to their job. And in many cases, former interns are among those employers look to first when filling vacancies for permanent employees.

Don't think that an internship is a rigid program that requires you to take a term off from school. Rather you can do an internship on a part-time basis—say, a few afternoons or evenings a week. You might do one in the summer time. Or

"Liberal education developes a sense of right, duty, and honor; and more and more in the modern world large business rests on rectitude and honor as well as on good judgement."

Educator Charles William Eliot

66

even use "junk time" that would otherwise be largely wasted such as three weeks between summer school and the fall term.

(4) Career Fairs.

These open house type events bring together employers who demonstrate their organizations and normal range of jobs with students looking for both information on careers and job opportunities. The advantage of a job fair is that in a few hours, you may look briefly at 15 to 25 organizations and identify several for later contact. The booths maintained by employers have representatives right there to answer any questions you may have.

Career Fairs are very common and may be sponsored by a group of colleges, by student groups, by a chamber of commerce, or by a regional association of employers. Once again, however, these will include far more large than small organizations, so use other techniques to make sure that you are in contact with the complete range of employment options.

(5) Employer Receptions.

Increasingly, organizations which recruit college students are arranging to meet informally through social receptions. These are like career fairs, except that only one employer is involved.

You would attend a reception in order to learn more about the company. However, the reception also has an evaluative element - the company representatives are looking you over, to see who they might invite for future interviews, either on campus or at the company offices. In any event, you will become more practiced at engaging business people and other employers if you attend many receptions and learn the social skills that are necessary in that setting.

(6) Alumni Networks.

Most colleges keep in touch with their graduates, perhaps more to raise money than for other reasons. But, increasingly alumni are being asked about their careers. What are their experiences after graduation? What advice can they give to today's students? And, do they have jobs in their organization which might be of interest to this year's seniors? Some colleges arrange meetings between graduating students and alumni who work in various metropolitan areas. The University of Virginia, for example, uses a Geographic Job Club to help provide such a linkage.

In other places, alumni volunteer to serve as career counselors, meeting with students who are home during vacation periods. They may refer them to other alumni for job leads. At one time, these may have been "old boy" networks but they have been expanded so that men and women of all socio-economic groups can take advantage of them.

Check with your school's career planning office and see if such a service is available to you.

"The people I work for told me they had no intention of hiring anybody when I first walked through the door, but after talking to me and reading my writing, they felt they would be making a mistake not to hire me."

Communications Executive, History Major

"The human mind is our fundamental resource."

President John F. Kennedy

67

(7) Career Counseling.

This might be one of the first steps in the process of making full use of the services open to you. Learn which office handles career counseling on your campus and you may want to review your plans, or make some if you haven't already, with the help of a trained counselor. Counselors can help you develop a clearer sense of career direction, consider how to decide among competing alternatives, and develop an action plan for reaching your goal. They may refer you to books, directories, or other people who may help.

Career counseling can be especially helpful when you feel knotted by indecision or when you are overwhelmed by having to cope with the job market. Good counselors usually try to help make your own decision rather than trying to prescribe what they think best. One of the great values of having thought through your career goals is that you can verbalize them better when taking job interviews later.

(8) Extern Programs.

These are similar to internships but are shorter in duration and are always unpaid. A common extern program places a student for a week or two with an employer, often an alumnus. These may be during an extended mid-year break or whenever the college program allows.

Extern programs allow students the opportunity to observe everyday life in an occupation and an actual employer. They are of particular value in providing a more realistic picture of a field than may be available from the outside and can help students make sure of a field before committing themselves to future coursework or deeper involvement. If your college does not have such a program, you may try to establish an externship on your own.

(9) Vocational Testing.

Standardized testing is often available in college career centers (or counseling centers) and private agencies away from the campus. Such testing usually proposes to help you establish a career direction, through assessment of your abilities, values, personality traits, interests, and other factors. While tests are widely available, they are not particularly good predictors of career choice and satisfaction. The student who obtains such test results should be careful about applying them to his/her career decisions. If a test seems to indicate that Accounting is right for you, or (more generally) that Business careers fit your test profile, ask yourself if you like business fields and if you believe you have some talent for them, before moving in that direction.

Just as importantly, do not rule yourself out of a career, even if test results don't indicate that direction for you. Assess your abilities and motivation based upon your past experiences. Ultimately, your assessment of yourself will be far more powerful and predictive than standardized testing.

Computer software programs such as DISCOVER, SIGI, and CHOICES have many of the features that appeal to those who favor testing but few of the liabilities. Through these programs you may self-assess your interests, values, and abilities and generate a variety of career options for further study.

(10) Employment Agencies.

Many people turn to fee-charging employment agencies each year. The lure of "someone who knows the job market better than I do" may be hard to resist. However, the key to using employment agencies is understanding how they operate. They have only certain jobs on file and will only make money if you take one of those positions. They may, therefore, oversell you on the virtues of a particular employer or on the values of entering a line of work which may never have occurred to you before.

Employment agencies are useful if you have recently entered an area and don't know much about its employers. Or you may see a job advertised by an agency which sounds especially appealing. But, keep in mind that agencies often advertise interesting jobs solely to get good candidates to register with them.

Most of these agencies only charge a fee it you take a job through their efforts. That is, a fee is charged to you if you accept one of their referrals to an employer and later accept his or her job. Fees may range from 6 to 12 percent of the first year's salary. You need to ascertain very carefully what costs are involved and how your liability is determined. In general, one should never pay an employment service a flat fee for "job hunting assistance" such a a $300 to $500 "registration" fee for its help.

Unlike college-based career conselors, employment agancies are in business to make money and they only make it when you take a job through their efforts. For this reason, they may refer you to jobs which are not great hoping that you will accept the position and pay their fee. In some cases, the employer may offer to pay the fee, which saves you money. But the agency is still going to benefit if you take the job— whether or not it is the best thing you might accept.

If you are new to an area, and know nothing about its employment agencies, you might call the Better Business Bureau for suggestions. At least, the Bureau might know of some that you should not touch. Or you might call a local college career placement service and ask for its recommendations concerning employment agencies in the area. The college might just say that it will help you, particularly if you happen to call outside of its busy season.

The important thing to remember is to proceed cautiously when using employment agencies. They can be an asset. They can also be a liability.

"Dartmouth is a small college, sir, but there are those who love it."

Senator Daniel Webster

(11) Other Sources.

There are many other individuals or networks which may assist you. You might get help from a women's center or a program specifically established to aid your racial or ethnic group.

Teachers or faculty members may help you identify potential employers. But, they can only help if they know you and your interests.

Finally, on almost every survey of employment assistance college graduates say that their families were the single most useful source of advice. So, make full use of advice, job leads or other help from your family. This means more than your immediate family, look at the help you might receive from relatives, close family friends, or neighbors.

For some reason, many students tend to downgrade their families as a source of help. As Mark Twain said "When I was seventeen, I felt father knew very little about life. Later, in my twenties, I was amazed at how much he had learned in just a few years."

CAREER PROFILE

"If you are confident of your ability to read, write, comprehend, and use numbers and have common sense, you can compete."

Leslie Geballe
BA Classics, 1969
Coordinator of Special Projects
Texas Governor's Office of Economic Development

Liberal Arts Education

A liberal arts background has been an asset and a satisfaction to me, professionally and personally. In my view, there is no adequate substitute for a broad undergraduate education that enables one to be comfortable with a variety of subjects, develops the ability to communicate orally and in writing, and establishes a frame of reference to give relevance and significance to many situations in the working world. The claim that liberal arts studies might offer a relevant context to the political and policy-laced world of the public sector probably ought to be defended, so let me suggest a couple of examples.

On any given day, I will engage in activities ranging from policy analysis (sometimes involving quantative analysis) to fact-finding, to speech and letter-writing, to planning, and responding to requests from individuals, communities, and businesses. Versatility and adaptability are important attributes, as is resourcefulness...knowing how to find an answer, or sometimes where to take the next step. One must be able to grasp a subject, even if superficially, sort out its vital aspects and quickly arrive at a recommendation or a plan of action. Any recommendation must be presented succinctly and clearly.

How does this relate to liberal arts? Liberal arts students study subjects ranging from science to history to literature. We have a short time to understand and achieve some level of competence in widely differing topics. We are experienced in diverse learning skills. In the study of English literature, for example, we may analyze a novel by chapter, by character development, or by minor themes. We know all along that the novel has a structure that gives a sense of order to isolated parts...that parts connect to the whole. In my work, I find that identifying and keeping hold of an organization concept avoids becoming mired in details.

Language courses, too, have proved their worth, not solely for the obvious reasons. The study of foreign languages taught me a profound understanding of how and why words fit together, an appreciation that was far more difficult to gain from the study of English alone. Since writing is a major part of my work, I place a high value on this aspect of education.

Job Search Techniques/Results

I originally obtained a position in the Governor's Office by following a personal contact. One of sixty-four applicants, I felt fortunate to be selected, although the position was temporary. I had worked long beyond the commitment - in fact, had forgotten that the employment was temporary, when I was informed that I had been made a permanent employee.

"Permanent" is, of course, a relative term in any position. In my position, longevity is a close relative of adaptability, not so much due to politics, but because staffs are small; work is diverse; "turnaround time" short; and specialization a luxury we can only partially afford. Liberal arts students tend to be versatile, and that can be an asset.

Job Advice

Confidence in a job search will come with defining your scope of interest and being realistic about opportunities. Clearly, if you have chosen a liberal arts path, you would not compete for highly technical jobs without seeking additional training in the field in question. I, in fact, did attend graduate school in public affairs, but having done so, I do not feel that it added appreciably to my ability to perform.

An employer will be interested in someone who is versatile, creative, and has good judgement, who will make reasoned decisions and who can figure out what must be done and how to do it. If you have done well in college, are confident of your ability to read, write, comprehend and use numbers AND have common sense, you can compete. These are the skills of a generalist; the liberal arts student has given him or herself a solid grounding in them and much practice applying them. Since you will be looking for an entry level job, employers will expect to train you in the specifics.

I recommend that job-seekers take their time in the job search. Think about what you will be doing on the job and where it will lead, either in that particular setting or others. Use personal contacts, talk with friends, to people they might suggest. Try to interview professionals in fields or companies that interest you and, above all, don't panic. It may take time, but you will succeed.

Section 11
References on Liberal Education and Careers

"Nothing is really work unless you would rather be doing something else."

Author Sir James Barrie

Here is an extensive summary of books, reports, and periodical articles dealing with liberal education and careers.

While the articles and studies tend to support the view that liberal arts graduates can compete for a wide variety of jobs and have a background that can contribute to long-term advancement in their careers, nothing in here should lead to the conclusion that there is "Nothing to worry about. Don't assume that liberal arts graduates will do just fine." There are very few givens in this life and liberal education does not automatically lead to anything. Murphy and Jenks noted, "liberal arts students expect employers to notice how wonderful they are," an attitude that will get any graduate in trouble, not just those with a general background. All college graduates must be prepared to sell themselves to employers. Jobs don't come to people, people seek out jobs. Furthermore, there is nothing so intrinsically superior about a liberal education that all of its graduates will gain a natural advantage in the marketplace.

This bibliography is not intended to defend the liberal arts degree. Liberal education will survive and prosper just fine on its own, since career success is only one of the desired outcomes of a liberal education. This list cites background sources which may help students, counselors, and others to assess the values of liberal education for themselves and to develop a background of knowledge which may help them as they select careers, explain the "why" of their academic program to employers, and otherwise move from the classroom to the workplace. One would hope, also, that students who are studying specialized subjects in college would also be encouraged to augment their major courses with subjects selected from the liberal arts curriculum. Engineers, lawyers, accountants, or other professionals can't expect to be fully successful if they focus narrowly on the entry tools of their trades.

If this bibliography proves anything it is that the skills of a liberal education are like a hidden curriculum which alert students find a way to acquire - one way or another. The problems of leadership in the workplace involve written and verbal communications, motivating and adjusting to the needs of diverse people, and studying and analyzing complex issues and situations. If liberal education did not exist, we would have to invent it.

Thus, themes inherent in these references are not telling us that one kind of education is better than another. That debate will range on long after these pages have turned to dust and tomorrow's scholars have retired. The message here is that college graduates can design new equipment, accounting

73

systems, or computer programs with great genius but they should not expect to move and shake companies if all they have to offer is technical expertise.

I would hope that the study of liberal education will give students some idea of how to grapple with the biggest, most complex problems we face today. As an illustration, the Japanese challenge to American business is not going to be solved solely by use of computers, ledger sheets, or even engineering prowess. This problem requires the study of a language, a culture, and an outlook on life quite different from our own. The sociology, the geography, the psychology, and the history of Japanese business and society all directly affect our own American balance of trade problems.

The references which follow should be viewed as a point-of-departure, not the final word. You don't have to believe any interpretation of the information or viewpoints which it includes. If you want to find out for yourself, use the list of references as a guide to formulating questions and types of contacts which may help you.

- Talk to business executives, such as those whose attitudes appear in many of the references.
- Talk to researchers in colleges and universities who have made studies of liberal arts alumni.
- Talk to recent graduates themselves and ask how their training has affected their careers.
- Make your own study of both employers and liberal arts alumni.

But until you gather better information through your own efforts, don't knock liberal education as preparation for work. The best evidence we have so far tells us that a liberal arts degree is as good as any other and, more often than not, in the long run it is better.

"Nothing kills sales more than dull products. People lead with their senses. We live to touch, feel, listen, and see. Our fundamental activity is communication. Scholastically, these senses are in the domain of the liberal arts."

Tom Jackson
"Wake Up, Corporate America"

Bibliography: Liberal Education and Careers

To help readers identify items of special interest, the following coding is used in the letter before each entry:

B - Business and Liberal Arts
C - Career Prospects for Liberal Arts Graduates
M - Liberal Arts Job Search Manuals
S - General Support of Liberal Education in the World of Work
D - Data Studies Relevant to Liberal Arts Graduates (LAG's)
J - Job Search for LAG's
CR - Liberal Arts as a Curriculum
MS - Miscellaneous

C - **Academic Preparation for the World of Work**, New York, The College Board, 1984.

S - "Are Liberal Arts Graduates Good for Anything?" John L. Munschauer. **The Chronicle of Higher Education,** September 10, 1979.

Munschauer says employers and students who ask "What good is liberal education?" are asking the wrong question. He suggests they ask questions such as "Should we know anything about religion, government, and the philosophies that influence us and the rest of the world?","Should we ground ourselves in the sciences as a basis for understanding the world around us?" He goes on to say, "Good Lord, why would a student want to spend his time dulling his mind on a boring course in salesmanship when this can be taught better by a good sales manager on the job?"

C - **Aside From Teaching English, What In The World Can You Do?** 2nd edition, Dorothy Bestor, Seattle, University of Washington Press, 1982.

An excellent book which reinforces the view that a liberal education can be applied across a wide spectrum in the world of work. Special attention is given to the careers that English majors and humanities students might want to pursue - publishing, teaching, technical writing, and media fields. The book also covers in detail career opportunities in business, consulting, and government, and entrepreneurship. A chapter entitled "Will a different degree help?" is enlightening. In all, the book shows numerous strong career options for literate college graduates and helps such grads determine how they can approach the job market most effectively.

B - "Broad-based Education Pays Best in Long Run." Lisa Aug. **USA Today**, April 21, 1986, p. E1.

S - "Back to the Liberal Arts!" Bill Sloan. **Dallas** Magazine, March, 1979.

The author cites examples of rising young business executives who fail to get promoted because their business studies in college did not give them sufficient breadth or ability to communicate. Citing a saying of Confucious ("He who knows something but knows not how to express it is as he who knows nothing"), he reports efforts in certain business school curricula (at Southern Methodist University, for example) to correct this deficiency.

B - "Building Bridges Between Business and Campus." Kathryn Mohrman. **Liberal Learning and Careers Series**. Washington, Association of American Colleges, 1983.

This publication summarizes the results of three conferences (held in Hartford, Memphis, and San Francisco Bay area) in which liberal arts faculty and business executives met to recommend ways to improve cooperation and understanding between business and higher education. This report describes the three conferences, presents the recommendations developed by participants, and concludes with suggestions for the replication of the model in other locations.

B - "Business Basics for Liberal Arts Graduates." Jane H. Cordisco and Janet L. Walker. **Journal of College Placement,** Spring 1983, pp. 18-19.

B - "Business Graduates too Narrow , Report Says", **Cam Report**, November 1, 1985, East Lansing, Michigan State University.

Prestigious graduate schools awarding master's degree in business are relying too heavily upon specialized courses and thus are not producing the well-rounded people that corporations desire, according to a report by the Business-Higher Education Forum, a group of corporate chief executives and university presidents. Recommendations included (a) competence in oral and written communication, (b) courses in "people management" - interviewing, counseling, negotiating, and disciplining, (c) more exposure to disciplines outside the business school for a 'better appreciation of the complex interrelationships that govern decisions in today's business.'

B - "Business Leadership and the Liberal Arts," David G. Winter, **New Jersey Bell Journal**, Volume 1, No. 3, 1978-79.

Readers who observe the superior performance by liberal arts graduates in corporations may ask, "what specific qualities enable them to advance in their organizations?" This is one of the few studies available which provides an answer. In the study conducted by Winter and his colleagues, respected social science researchers at McBer and Company, liberal arts students were compared with others in terms of intellectual skills and qualities of mind. "The ability to argue both sides of a complex, controversial issue" is an example of such a skill. These qualities, possessed in greater abundance by liberal arts students are associated with effective performance by business managers.

B - "Business and Liberal Arts: A Perfect Pail?" Jean C. Wyer. **National Business Employment Weekly**, College Careers Edition, Fall 1984, pp. 27-28.

B - "Business More Receptive to Liberal Arts," **New York Times**, Gene I. Maeroff, June 23, 1981.

Maeroff summarizes what was at the time an emerging trend, business leaders are coming to appreciate an education that at its best produces graduates who can write and think clearly and solve problems—even it if takes them longer to become conversant with some vocational techniques."

B - "Can Engineers Succeed in General Management?" 1983 IEEE Careers Conference, Ann Howard, AT&T.

In answer to the question posed in the title of this paper, Ms. Howard reports the results of a Bell System study and says: "Some certainly can and do, but in managerial skills, on the average, they come up a little short compared to other majors. Although skills and understanding can't be underrated...the higher one goes in the hierarchy, the less important they become."

C - "Career Advice for Liberal Arts Students," John L. Munschauer. **Business Week's Guide to Careers**, February/March, 1984.

In this article, Munschauer stresses that liberal arts students do not limit themselves to campus recruitment programs in their search for jobs: "Job opportunities in fields such as import/export, advertising, publishing, politics, small retail stores,...travel or fine arts will probably not be found through the oncampus recruitment process.

B - "A Career Interview Program; For Liberal Arts Students Seeking Business Careers." Jeff W. Garis and H. Richard Hess. **Journal of College Placement**, Winter 1985, pp. 39-42.

C - "Career Pathways: A Conference for Liberal Arts Students." Paula Hoffman Lowe and Daisy E. Virgil. **Journal of College Placement**, Winter 1983, pp. 38-42.

C - **Career Patterns of Liberal Arts Graduates,** Robert Calvert, Jr. Cranston, RI: The Carroll Press, 1969. This book reports on one of the most comprehensive studies ever made of liberal arts alumni. It surveyed 11,000 graduates from 108 colleges and universities who were five, ten, and fifteen years out of college. The survey asked a number of questions about the cultural lives, the careers, and their general satisfaction with their own liberal arts training. The overall conclusion was that the graduates were satisfied with their educational preparation and would, if they had to do it all over again, repeat liberal arts training.

D - **"Career Status and Satisfaction of Recent Business and Arts/Humanities College Graduates** Alyce C. Martinez, William E Sedlacek, Thomas D. Bachhuber, University of Maryland, 1983.

C - "Careers in Data Processing - For the Liberal Arts Major." Lorett Treese. **The Collegiate Career Women**, Spring 1985, pp. 37-39.

C - **Careers for Graduates in History** (chart). Germantown, MD: National Center for the Study of History, 1984.

An excellent and detailed chart describing numerous careers available to history majors, distributed across teaching and education, private nonprofit organizations, private individual or small firms, public agencies, and private sector corporations. Typical employers and specific job duties are described for approximately 40 different areas of work.

D - **Careers of Humanities College Graduates**, California State University, Long Beach, Career Planning and Placement Office, 1984.

C - **Careers in Information Management**, (chart) Germantown, MD. National Center for the Study of History, 1986.

This chart was prepared for graduates in the liberal arts with special reference to historians. It describes in detail 38 different "information management" career fields, under the broad headings of archives and records management, information science, library science, multi-disciplinary research, and museum curatorship. It also includes a table of over 250 job titles in these fields.

M - Careers in Transition: The Special Challenge for the Liberal Arts and Sciences Student in the Eighties, Barbara Seidman and Bill Kenzler, Career Development and Placement Center, Urbana-Champaign, University of Illinois, 1980.

A 200-page manual designed to assist the liberal arts student in understanding his or her opportunities in the job market. The most helpful sections include case studies of recent graduates and their transitions to the world of work, advice from employers, typical entry-level jobs, an assessment of liberal arts skills, guidelines for investigating the world of work, recommended methods for gaining experience outside the classroom, and compendium of the most commonly asked questions about career planning and job hunting.

J - Careers Without Reschooling: The Survival Guide to the Job Hunt for Liberal Arts Graduates. Dick Goldberg. Riverside, NJ; Crossroads/Continuum, 1985.

The opening chapter is an interview with Richard Bolles in which he explains how a liberal arts student can get over the hurdle of feeling he or she has little to offer in the marketplace. In subsequent chapters several problems of the graduate job search are identified and given attention—identifying marketable skills, tapping the hidden job market, writing a clear resume, and getting the interviewer to want you. These are major concerns for ALL job-hunters, of course, but the chapter authors explain how liberal arts graduates are especially susceptible to these problems and how they can solve them. The last 60% of the book consists of very readable interviews with professionals in 13 different areas of work that are populated with liberal arts alumni.

MS - "The Case Against Credentialism," James Fallows. **The Atlantic Monthly**, December, 1985.

The author charges that having academic credentials, though highly valued in the "meritocracy" we live in, is not related to competence in one's work or chosen profession: "they (credentials) are simultaneously too restrictive and too lax. They are too restrictive in giving a huge advantage to those who booked an early passage on the IQ train and too lax in their sloppy relation to the skills that truly make for competence." (If sports were run like the meritocracy, the Miami Dolphins would choose their starting lineup on the basis of...who had the highest proportion of 'quick-twich' fibers)." He cites examples of competence testing in industry to support his ideas. By implication, a liberal education is just as good as one that is vocationally specific, and perhaps better if it enables the person to do a better job.

D - "The Class of '77- One Year After Graduation," Daniel Hecker. **Occupational Outlook Quarterly,** Summer, 1982.

This study of 7,500 people who received bachelor's degrees shows the proportion of graduates for each field of study who were working in jobs generally requiring a college degree. Thus, for accounting, agriculture, art, and numerous other fields of study you have an operational definition of "underemployment". Also, the data shows proportions of graduates working in jobs that are related to their fields of study. The data were gathered only a few months after graduation. Percentage employed and percentage in graduate school are also given for each field of study. The proportion of graduates working in jobs related to their majors varied widely from one academic area to another. The technical areas (engineering, accounting, etc.) tended to have higher proportions, and the liberal arts areas (humanities and social sciences) tended to have lower proportions.

B - The Classic Touch: Lessons in Leadership from Homer to Hemingway. John K. Clemens and Douglas F. Mayer. Dow Jones Irwin, Homewood, Illinois, 1987.

This unique book draws parallels between classic literature and the problems of modern management. For example, Plato's Republic is viewed as an exemplary CEO reshaping his organization to produce superior results. Shakespeare's Macbeth details the agonies of blind ambition. King Lear is a study of the problem that powerful leaders have in allowing themselves successors. Willy Loman is Everyperson's fear of failure and following a false dream. Agamemnon and Achilles demonstrate how egotism can tear down a well-designed plan and sabotage the best of skills. John Stuart Mill set the standard for understanding participative leadership. Darwin's Origin of Species has lessons regarding "adaptability" that could benefit companies trying to change in the face of new market needs. And so it goes. The dilemmas of modern management have been faced before by writers with wisdom and eloquence. Leadership problems are not new. The timeless literature can help today's executives see "the big picture" more fully. Universal ideas help us to look beyond faddish or present-bound managerial theories. Clemens and Mayer are professors of management. They offer every manager the opportunity to expand his/her vision through reading books they may have thought were only for undergraduates.

C - "The College Curriculum and the Marketplace," Roger L. Geiger, **Change,** November/ December, 1980.

D - "College Experiences and Managerial Performance," Ann Howard, **Journal of Applied Psychology**, 1986, Volume 71, No. 3.

In an update of the classic study done at AT&T by Robert Beck, the author finds similar conclusions. On every scale measured—Abilities (Administrative, Interpersonal, Intellectual), Motivation (Advancement, Work Involvement), and Personality (Stability, Independence, Nonconformity)— Humanities and Social Science graduates surpassed Math/Science, Business, and Engineering graduates. The author indicates that communication skills and interpersonal skills are the best predictors of success in business; hence one would expect liberal arts graduates to have considerable promise in the business world, if the AT&T results are generalizable to a variety of corporations.

CR - **College Majors and Careers: A Resource Guide for Effective Life Planning,** Paul Phifer. Garrett Park, MD: Garrett Park Press, 1987. The author, a career resources director, points out the interests, aptitudes, and skills often associated with each of 60 college majors. Each major is defined and illustrative kinds of work toward which it may lead are cited. Unlike many books on careers, this book emphasizes the role of one's personal values in making life plans.

C - "Communications: Signals Are 'Go.'" Dan Hulbert, Careers: Occupational Outlook Section of **New York Times**, October 12, 1980.

B - "Computer Specialists are Singing the Blues" A Greater Stress on Human Side, Less on Technical Urged," Elizabeth M. Fowler, **New York Times**, March 25, 1984.

Fowler reports that many corporations found many of their information science specialists inadequately trained in human relations skills to advance to positions of managerial responsibility. A liberal arts student can read this as an opportunity to combine his/her greater sensitivity to interpersonal relations with computer courses and/or experience, and therefore offer the combination of talents that businesses are looking for.

M - **Consider Your Options: Business Opportunities for Liberal Arts Graduates**. Christine A. Gould, Washington, Association of American Colleges, 1983.

This is a job search manual for use by liberal arts students who want to pursue jobs and careers in the business world. It consists of four parts: (a) a survey of college recruiters indicating the qualities they seek in job applicants, (b) full-page statements by liberal arts graduates who have found rewarding careers in business, (c) advice on the job search process from a variety of sources (sample resumes are included), (d) profiles of 24 corporations which responded to the survey.

B - "Corporate Training and the Liberal Arts," Norman R. Smith, **Phi Delta Kappan**, January, 1980.

This article expands on John Henry Cardinal Newman's thesis that a liberal education is highly "useful" and practical in the world of work, particularly in terms of an individual's ability to absorb corporate training programs and translate them into gains for the organization. Thus, the ability to learn is applied to both technical subjects and the more far-reaching concerns of company goals and policies. The same mind that learns what a new computer can do also imagines how the computer may affect the company's future.

CR - "Curriculum Counts - For Liberal Arts Students Seeking Business Careers." Jeff W. Garis, H. Richard Hess, and Deborah J. Marron. **Journal of College Placement**, Winter 1985, pp. 32-37.

A survey of employers reveals their attitudes toward liberal arts graduates who complete a business minor. Overall, they feel this is a favorable curricular combination and that it will have positive effect on one's employment. The study also reveals that "communication/interpersonal skills" are by far the attributes most frequently cited by employers in selection decisions after campus interviews.

S - "Dirty Words: Leadership and Liberal Learning," Frederick Rudolph. **Change** magazine, April, 1980.

The author asserts that "curricular design has become largely a matter of baiting traps for students in a competitive effort to build departmental enrollments". He insists that liberal education is necessary as a balance to vocationally-oriented programs to introduce a sense of valuing: "The most magnificently trained doctor can actually be injurious to our psychological well-being. Technical competence cannot compensate for human indifference."

B - "Do Corporations Really Want Liberal Arts Grads?" Emanuel Sturman, **Management Review**, September, 1986.

Sturman outlines an essential problem that liberal arts graduates face when seeking entry-level jobs—middle-managers who hire often look for specialized "skills," while higher-level executives in their own companies prefer liberal arts graduates. He offers numerous quotes from company officials that attest to this situation. We might call this employer-speaking-with-forked-tongue. Sturman wants graduates to know this reality, and offers suggestions about how they can deal with it successfully.

D - **Early Career Patterns of Humanities College Graduates: One's Institution's Perspective of the "Lean Years," 1972 - 1981**. David S. Bechtel, Career Development and Placement Center, University of Illinois, Urbana, 1984.

MJ - "Early Employment Situations and Work Role Satisfaction among Recent College Graduates", Ellen W. Richards, **Journal of Vocational Behavior**, 24 (3), 305-318 (1984).

B - **Educating Managers: Executive Effectiveness through Liberal Learning**. Joseph Johnston, Jr. editor. Washington. Association of American Colleges, 1986.

"This book is written by a team of business executives, management scholars, business and liberal arts faculty, and academic administrators...(who have) been directly involved in efforts to win a central place for liberal learning in the development of business managers"..." It urges a central role for liberal learning in the development of current and future managers as a matter of simple good sense and enlightened self-interest on the part of businesses and those who lead them." The chapter entitled "What the Research Shows" is an outstanding summary and synthesis of numerous studies that examine the managerial value of a liberal education. Themes of other chapters include the skills that management needs from higher education, conversations with prominent executives, liberal learning and undergraduate business study, and recommendations for academic and business leaders. In all, this book clarifies both the good and the bad in liberal learning's relationship to management, and points out the way toward improving the understanding between liberal educators and business managers.

B - "Educating Tomorrow's Managers: Liberal Arts or Business School?" Doris Unger. **Professional Training**, Winter, 1985 1,12.

B - Education for Business: A Reassessment." Judd H. Alexander, **Wall Street Journal**, February 2, 1981, p.16.

A prominent executive reports his company's shift to include liberal arts graduates in their hiring on the assumption that they contribute greatly to the company's long-range potential because of their leadership qualities. The company wants graduates who are visionary, historical in their outlook, versatile, and effective communicators, in addition to graduates who have entry-level business skills. Alexander echoes the oft-heard thought that business education is far less important than the ability to learn, the drive toward excellence, and the ability to analyze the problems of a business from a long-range perspective.

MJ - "Education for Work", Barbara S. Uehling, **Journal of College Placement**, Summer 1979.

C - **The Educational Implications of High Technology**, Henry M. Levin and Russell W. Rumberger, Palo Alto, School of Education, Stanford University, February, 1983.

The authors contradict the popular belief that technological jobs will dominate future labor markets. They indicate that only 7% of new jobs will be "high technology" jobs, and conclude that "the educational system will strengthen the analytical and communicative skills of students, because such skills will help them deal with the changing political, economic, social and cultural institutions they will face in their adult lives."

C - "Emphasis Returns to Liberal Arts," **Sacramento Bee**, January 18,1987 (New York Times Service).

"At a time when the world is becoming more technical, there appears to be growing support for a swing back to the liberal arts...G.C. Parker, professor of management at Stanford University's graduate business school, said recently that 'the well-prepared manager of next generation will simply need more than the nation's graduate schools of business can provide...Managers in the next century must understand foreign cultures, languages, politics, and business practices'." Also, James Gibbons, Stanford's Dean of the School of Engineering said: "most important issues have qualitative and subjective dimensions which are best approached through study of literature, history, art, and social sciences."

S - "Environment Writers Need Liberal Arts More than Writing," Rodger Streitmatter. **Journalism Educator**, Autumn, 1984

"Students who want to become environmental reporters should not major in journalism or natural sciences. Instead, they should seek a broad liberal arts education with no more than a smattering of science and writing courses. This advice comes from a survey of 24 print and broadcast environment reporters representing the country's largest newspapers, TV networks, news magazines, and wire services". The article contains an explanation of these results and examples of how a broad education helps on the job.

B - "Ethics in America's Money Culture." Felix Rohatyn, **New York Times**, June 3, 1987.

Rohatyn, a prominent investment banker, urges businesses to draw their leaders from graduates of the liberal arts. He says, "what is desperately needed in an increasingly complex world dominated by technicians is the skepticism and the sense of history that a liberal arts education provides. History, philosophy, logic, English literature are more important to deal with today's problems than great technical competence." He emphasizes that the creativity of great scientific minds must be combined with the ethical judgment needed to make sound and humane decisions.

CR - "Faculty Roles in Career Advising of Liberal Arts Students." David R. Hiley. **Liberal Learning and Career Series**. Washington, Association of American Colleges, 1982.

Hiley states initially: "The weakest link between liberal arts students and the work world is the liberal arts faculty" and there are few who would argue strenuously against this. He explains some of the barriers to faculty involvement, but then recommends ways the institution can change to involve faculty more fully. He concludes by citing several colleges that have developed links between faculty and the career planning and placement services.

B - "The Failure of Business Education - and What to do About It, " Edward J. Mandt. **Management Review**, August, 1982.

The author urges that business schools incorporate more liberal education into their curricula. He says, "The typical business school curriculum fails to prepare students properly. It fills the student's head with facts and specialized theory. But neither of these is integrated into any kind of cohesive system...technicians' education...often is an accumulation of solutions to yesterday's problems. The rate at which the world changes prevents schools from keeping their technical curricula current." He adds, "What the newcomer should bring to the job is an insight into human behavior, the ability to think clearly and systematically, and the skill to communicate. Supervisors must ask themselves if their current crop of new employees possesses these attributes to any significant degree. Most likely they would answer in the negative."

M - **For Your Action: A Practical Job-Search Guide for the Liberal Arts Student**. Wayne Wallace, Carol French Wagner, Nancy Pentecost, and Pam Houston. Bloomington, IN: Arts and Sciences Placement Office, Indiana University, 1982.

A very detailed job search manual for liberal arts students, written by the professional staff of one of the best university career planning and placement centers. Many of the best resource materials from the Indiana U. career center are incorporated here, including samples of many kinds of correspondence with employers, resume examples, employment interviewing guidelines, forms for evaluating job offers, and many others. Sections on applying to graduate school, seeking summer jobs, and cautions about employment agencies are also included.

M - "From English Student to Professional - Through Resume Writing." Kenneth E. Jacobsen, Theodore R. Hovet, and Grace Ann Hovet. **Journal of College Placement,** Winter 1985, pp.44-47.

B - **From Student to Banker: Observations from the Chase Bank**. Burns, Stanley. Washington: Association of American Colleges, 1983.

In a study of recently hired "relationship managers" at Chase Manhattan (responsible for overseeing the bank's work with customers), Burns found that 60% of the low performers held MBA's, while 60% of the high performers held Bachelor of Arts degrees. Thus, from the start, liberally educated new managers without prior business training often perform as well or better than those with extensive formal training in business administration (the MBA's).

C - "The Future of the Generalist." Jay Rosson. **Journal of College Placement**, Summer 1980, pp. 59-60.

B - "Getting the Business: Doing Business with the Liberal Arts Degree." Betsey Todt Schmitt **Daily Herald** (Arlington Heights, I1), June 6, 1984.

J - **Getting a Job - What Skills Are Needed?**, Carol Murphy and Lynn Jenks. San Francisco: Far West Laboratories for Educational Research and Development, November 1982.

This is an extensive analysis of skills desired by employers. The critical difference in hiring is said to be the applicant's non-technical skills. The top ten functional skills (communication, writing, verbal, etc.) and the top ten adaptive skills (tactful, assertive, outgoing, etc.) are cited. Employers offer advice to educators about skill development, and the authors suggest general guidelines for enhancing the job-related skills of college students, They emphasize the importance (relevant to skill development) of classroom discussions, essay exams, term papers, definite deadlines, oral presentations, and group work.

S - "Go Ahead, Major in the Liberal Arts," by William J. Bennett. **Washington Post**, January 13, 1985.

The U.S. Secretary of Education writes about the importance of liberal arts in gaining employment, citing a study by the U. of Texas at Austin, that shows liberal arts graduates employed successfully in a wide variety of professions. Bennett highlights the U.T. conclusion; every product or service still requires people to sell the product, people to distribute the product, people to talk with those who use the product, and people to analyze markets for similar products." Bennett says to college students: "Do not fear the world too much. Take the time to make mankind your business."

S - "Grading the effects of a liberal arts education," David Winter, Abigail Stewart, and David McClelland. **Psychology Today**, September, 1978.

According to the results of specific measures administered to students of several different kinds of colleges: "students trained in the liberal arts are better able to formulate valid concepts, analyze arguments, define themselves, and orient themselves maturely to their world. The liberal arts education in at least one college also seems to increase the leadership motivation pattern - a desire for power, tempered by self-control."

B - "A Group Profile of The Fortune 500 Chief Executive." Charles G. Burck, **Fortune**, May, 1976.

A study of Fortune 500 CEO's showed 50% received their undergraduate degrees in liberal arts fields. Of these, economics degrees were the most frequent (26%), followed by humanities (17%), and then social sciences (7%).

C - **The High-Tech Career Guide,** Betsy Collard. Palo Alto, Women's Resource Group, 1985.

Perhaps the most detailed compilation of job titles and job descriptions in technological organizations in any career book available today. It turns out that most organizations are technological in some way, and yet many of the jobs in these companies or agencies are available to non-technical college graduates. Thus, this book might well have been titled the same as O'Brien's book immediately below. In 267 pages, Collard spells out hundreds of job descriptions in "functional areas" (engineering, marketing, sales and service, operations, materials, finance, management information systems, and human resources) and in other areas - writing, training, graphics, and public relations. She has thus balanced the areas of work that liberal arts graduates ask most about - i.e. public relations and human resources - with the many other areas of job opportunities that they know almost nothing about. Chapters on "How to learn more about companies and jobs" and "High-tech industries and trends" are also exceptionally helpful. This is a must-read book for any college graduate (especially those in liberal arts) who wants to expand his or her number of job possibilities and be well-informed before starting a job search.

C - **High-Tech Jobs for Non-Tech Grads**. Mark O'Brien. Englewood Cliffs, Nj: Prentice-Hall, Inc, 1986.

A 108-page book written by a former securities analyst and college career placement officer, this little book packs a lot of information into its pages, plus much sound advice. The author tells us the language of "high-tech," the specific jobs (with descriptions) a non-technical graduate can expect to compete for, and how to get a good start in this complex of industries. "How to find the right high-tech company" and "How to pick the winning from the losing high-tech company" are especially helpful chapters. This book provides much support for liberal arts graduates who want to work for technological organizations. Jobs are available and non-technical skills are in demand. O'Brien tells the graduates how to take full advantage of their background.

CR - "Higher Education or Higher Skilling?" Steven Muller, **Daedulas**, the **Journal of the American Academy of Arts and Sciences,** Fall 1974.

CR - **History as the Core of the Liberal Arts**, Paul J. Devendittis, Nassau Community College, Jan 16, 1980.

B - "The Humanist as Business Executive: Wishful Thinking?" Lewis Solmon. **Education Record**, 64(1), 32-37.

The author discusses the relevance of graduate study in the humanities to success in the business world. He points out that PhD. humanists can and often do succeed as business executives, but that it is false reasoning to think they succeed because of their humanities background.

B - **Humanities and Business: The Twain Shall Meet, But How?,** Roger B. Smith, Chairman of the Board, General Motors Corp., May 21, 1984.

B - "Humanities Offer Valuable Help for Grads in Business Careers." **Spotlight** (College Placement Council), January 1984, p.1.

MS - "I Tell Them I'm a Liberal Arts Major." Carol Jin Evans. **Chronicle of Higher Education.**

A beautiful poem about a liberal arts student beset by parents and peers who ask (of her liberal arts degree): "But, what are you going to DO with that?" She answers with sarcasm, and then, more seriously, in terms of the depths she has plumbed as a liberal art student. Her images provide a ringing endorsement for education as it enhances the growth of the individual.

B - "The Ideal Job Candidate for Large Insurance Companies is the Liberal Arts Graduate." **Spotlight** (College Placement Council), February 1985, p.2.

MS - "In Search of a Job," James Lileks. **Minnesota**, May/June, 1984.

"There are two kinds of jobs for liberal arts graduates: few and far between...you may have just received four years of vigorous education, but if you keep it to yourself no one will hold it against you." This is a humorous view of "selling" the liberal arts degree. It offers numerous suggestions regarding how to market specific major fields. It concludes by saying: "One of our own will get into power someday. The vote will be given only to those who, say, have finished Moby Dick. Then you'll see some changes around here."

B - "An Interview with John C. Sawhill," **Forbes**, November 12, 1979.

Sawhill, president of New York University, blames the ineffective communication among business, government, and society upon the nearly two decades of overspecialization in the curricula of U.S. colleges and universities. He explains that this specialization has spilled into corporations hiring policies, with the result that new graduates are often short-sighted in their perspectives. He cites as an example: "We find corporations, like those in the oil industry, who aren't able to respond effectively to criticism from consumer groups, environmentalists, a wide range of people in society." He states: "It is an advantage to a corporation to hire people with a broad general education and have the corporations supply the training."

C - "Job Sources for Liberal Arts Graduates," John William Zehring, **Journal of College Placement,** Winter 1979.

J - Jobs for English Majors and Other Smart People. 2nd edition, John L. Munschauer. Princeton, NJ: Peterson's Guides, Inc., 1986.

This book makes the important distinction between "professional work"—which must be trained for in law schools, engineering school, medical school, architecture school, and others—and "trait-oriented work" in which people are hired because they possess the right traits—such as communicative ability, sound judgement, reasoning skill, and imagination. The majority of jobs available to college graduates are "trait-oriented" and can be sought by liberal arts graduates as well as other grads. Munschauer tells insightful stories about liberal arts graduates who have used their personal qualities to gain success and reveals many principles for marketing oneself with a liberal arts degree. The book is an upbeat, entertaining, and highly practical job search manual. The author stresses imagination and persistence in job-hunting and gives much anecdotal proof that these qualities pay off.

B - "Let's Hear it for Liberal Arts," John A. Byrne. **Forbes**, July 1, 1985.

This prominent business journal reports that liberal arts graduates are receiving starting salaries in the $40,000 - 60,000 range from investment banking firms such as First Boston and Salomon Brothers. Big Eight accounting firms, consumer product organizations, and consulting firms are making big offers as well. The article points out that First Boston hired 90% of its new financial analysts from liberal arts programs. Apparently, in their search for "the best and the brightest," many companies expect to find them among liberal arts seniors. Often they would prefer to pay the new B.A. well, rather than offering the same dollars to a new M.B.A., because they can train the liberal arts graduates themselves.

C - "Liberal Arts and Careers: Taking the Long View." Annette Woodlief, **Journal of College Placement**, Summer, 1982, pp. 24-28.

CR - "Liberal Arts Colleges Bow to the Future." Lucia Solorzano. **U.S. News & World Report**, May, 23, 1983, p. 67.

The recent trend toward "vocationalizing" the liberal arts curriculum is described, with numerous colleges given as examples. The increasing presence of business programs, technical courses, and vocationally-focused majors in liberal arts colleges is seen as the inevitable movement of higher education toward a technology-oriented nation.

MS - The Liberal Arts: Colleges and Employers in Cooperation. Carol Shiner Wilson, Commission on Career Counseling and Placement, American College Personnel Association, 1985.

A summary of programs at 14 colleges and universities which address the needs of liberal arts students who seek a better understanding of their employment prospects. Each college approaches the problem differently and offers a different kind of assistance to the student, so the reader can benefit by knowing about all of these programs.

C - "Liberal Arts Colleges and Teacher Quality (What! Waste Your Dartmouth Education on a Career in Teaching?)." **American Educator**, 8(3), 18-21.

J - "The Liberal Arts Employment Dilemma." J.K. Hillstrom, **Journal of College Placement**, Spring, 1984.

The author explains five reasons why liberal arts graduates often have difficulty in the job market: (a) lack of salable skills, (b) lack of commitment to a chosen field of work, (c) unrealistically high expectations, (d) an attitude of snobbishness or being "above it all", (e) an unawareness of the profit-making nature of business enterprises. Hillstrom is right that liberal arts graduates often fall prey to these problems. He believes that a liberal education is inherently valuable in jobs and careers, but cautions graduates not to expect employers to recognize how wonderful they are.

B - "Liberal Arts in the Executive Suite." Thomas H. Wyman. **Journal of Career Planning and Employment**, Winter 1986, pp. 34-37.

C - "Liberal Arts Find a Degree of Recovery." Jim Gallagher. **Chicago Tribune**, May 29, 1984.

C - "Liberal Arts Graduates Move Ahead in the Job Market." **Career News Network**, University of Texas at Austin Career Center, Fall, 1984.

B - "Liberal Arts Graduates' Prospects in the Job Market Grow Brighter." Linda M. Watkins. **Wall Street Journal,** May 6, 1986, p.29.

According to the Journal, "Big employers are wooing liberal arts graduates with growing fervor, and the students are more receptive to corporate offers than their counterparts were a few years ago." Two key reasons are cited for this trend: (1) "After years of favoring job applicants with technical degrees, more employers are short on younger workers with more general analytical and writing skills." (2) "Liberal arts graduates are cheaper to hire than many other kinds." The flexibility of a liberal education and breadth of his or her viewpoint are emphasized in this article. Several corporations— Peat-Marwick-Mitchell, Needham-Harper-Worldwide, Digital Equipment Corp., and others— explain why they often prefer liberal arts alumni. Peat-Marwick says that liberal arts graduates bring a global outlook that makes them more receptive to international assignments.

C - "Liberal Arts Graduates Find Themselves Back in Demand." Beth Arburn Davis. **Corpus Christi Caller Times**, October 6, 1985.

The recent resurgence of interest in liberal arts graduates is attributed to their people skills and generic learning skills, which are increasingly useful in an unpredictable economy. A dean of Corpus Christi University says: "The accountant will probably get the job at the bank first, but who's going to become the president?"

M - **Liberal Arts Job Search: A Guide for Successful Self-Placement in the Job Market**. Sande Raye Schrier. Austin, Career Center of the University of Texas, 1985.

A 42-page manual describing the results of a survey of U. of Texas liberal arts graduates, which includes several articles explaining the qualities of liberal arts graduates that are desired in the job market. A feature of the manual is a set of liberal arts alumni profiles, in which graduates explain how their liberal eduction has affected their career progress. The manual emphasized self-placement, rather than reliance upon the campus recruitment programs, and other specific guidelines for the job search.

C - **Liberal Arts Jobs**. Burton Jay Nadler. Princeton, NJ: Peterson's Guides, Inc. 1986.

Over 300 career fields and job descriptions for liberal arts graduates are included here. Each job or career area is defined in great detail, with typical places of employment, methods of entry, and patterns of advancement within that field. The descriptions are very readable and realistic and provide a clear picture of the nature of work. Used in combination with Collard's High Tech Career Guide and Life After Shakespeare, these three books offer the liberal arts graduate all the career options he or she could ever want.

S - "Liberal Arts Light Pat Into Future", by James Michener, **Austin American Statesman**, Oct. 28, 1984.

B - **Tne Liberal Arts Major in Bell System Management**. Beck, Robert E., Washington, DC: Association of American Colleges, 1981.

At the time, the Bell System employed more than 5,000 college graduates, of which 1/3 were liberal arts graduates. In this presentation, Beck reports from the ongoing longitudinal research which Bell conducts on its managers. This is one of the few longitudinal studies comparing liberal arts graduates with the progress of other majors in the business community. Results showed that 43% of them advanced to the fourth level of management (considered senior management status), compared to 32% of business graduates and 23% of engineering graduates. He further reports: "The humanities/ social sciences majors showed especially strong interpersonal skills and were similar to business majors in administrative skills and motivation for advancement. Their greatest weakness was in quantitative skills."

B - "Liberal Arts Majors Prove Specialization Isn't Required for Success in Business," Sam Bittner, **Chronicle of Higher Education,** April 14, 1982, page 25.

One example is worth a thousand lofty statements. The author reports: "I hired a student from Stanford University who was home for the summer. He was majoring in Latin American history with a minor in philosophy. I gave him an airplane ticket and a credit card and told him: 'Go to Denver and research the Bureau of Mines archives and locate a chemical process for the recovery of beryllium.' He left on Monday. I forget to tell him that I was sending him for the impossible. He came back on Friday…and said: 'Here is the process. It was developed 33 years ago at a government research station at Rolla, MO…and here also are other processes for the recovery of mica, strontium, columbiam, and yttrium, which also exist as residual ores that contain beryllium.'" The author goes on to say: "If we continue with the present trend of specialized education, we are going to be successful in keeping a steady supply of drones moving to a huge beehive. Our country was not built by a bunch of drones. It was built by people."

S - "Liberal Arts Make Cents," Diane Petzke, **East Side Express,** New York, NY, Oct. 21, 1984.

C - "Liberal Arts and Middle Managers." Joseph S. Johnston. **Reports: The Journal of the Association of Governing Boards of Universities and Colleges**, July/August, 1985, pp.10-11.

J - **Liberal Arts Power!** Burton Nadler. Princeton, NJ, Peterson's Guides, Inc., 1985.

A book which focuses on the development of resumes for liberal arts graduates. In an impressive array of examples the author does an outstanding job of showing how coursework, out-of-class experiences, and career goals can be intertwined and made into resumes that are coherent and strong selling tools. The stories behind the resumes are the magic in this book. They will give liberal arts graduates confidence to tell their own stories in effective ways. The book leaves a reader with the impression that any liberal arts graduate who examines his or her background closely can create a resume that will enliven his or her job search and be well-received by employers.

CR - **Liberal Arts Skills**. Paul Breen and Urban Whitaker. The Learning Center, P.O. Box 27616, San Francisco, CA, 1982.

Brief definitions of 76 generic skills that are applicable to many different problem-solving and task-oriented situations. This is an excellent inventory of skills for liberal arts job-hunters who want to assess themselves and develop a vocabulary for describing their unique strengths. The skills, developed in consultation with students, faculty, and employers, are organized into nine major groups: "Information Management," "Valuing," "Communication," "Research and Investigation," "Critical Thinking," "Design and Planning," "Management and Administration," "Human Relations," and "Personal/Career Development."

B - "Liberal Arts Students and Their Skills," Mary J. Hicks, Stephen Koller, and Nancy Tellett-Royce. **Journal of College Placement**, Spring, 1984.

Eighty-nine business employers in Minnesota indicated on a survey the kinds of skills they value most in entry-level job candidates. Concurrently, 30 academic departments from liberal arts colleges were asked about the kinds of skills they judge to be acquired by their students. Comparing the results from these two sources, the authors found many similarities between what employers say they want and the skills that liberal arts faculty say their students possess. Research of this kind may help encourage a common language between academicians and employers, so that links between education and work might become more clear.

B - "Liberal Arts is Useful Training for Management." Stanley F. Paulson **The Evening News**, Harrisburg, PA, October 2, 1981, page 19.

The author summarizes several studies which provide evidence that the liberal education is relevant to the success of many people in the management world. He refers in detail to a study done by Pennsylvania State University, (where he was Dean of the College of Liberal Arts at the time), which revealed that liberal arts graduates were more successful than their counterparts in specialized curricula: "Over a period of time ranging from three to 14 years,…they (liberal arts graduates) outdistanced the field…in salaries and presumably in value to their organizations."

C - "Liberal, not Vocational Skills." Howard E. Figler. **Alumnus** magazine, Dickinson College, February, 1976.

The author describes the skills (communication, thinking, human relations, valuing, investigative, interviewing) and attributes (making decisions based on partial information, interpreting foreign tongues, mediating between interest groups, dealing with the unknowable) that are most crucial in job and career success, and claims that these can be acquired best from a liberal education. He cautions parents of college students not to demand vocationally-specific programs, because these will be less valuable in the long run. He explains that a liberal education helps prepare a student for a career, a life's work, rather than for a beginning job.

B - "The Liberally Educated Graduate in Corporate Management." Michael Useem in **Educating Managers: Executive Effectiveness Through Liberal Learning**, edited by Joesph Johnston, San Francisco, Jossey-Bass, 1986.

This lengthy chapter is the best available summary of research relevant to the effects of liberal education in the corporate world. Summarizing more than 50 studies, Useem finds much evidence that liberal education is valued in businesses. He does not, however, conclude that a liberal arts degree is necessarily the best preparation for corporate management. He indicates that liberal education can be acquired in certain business education programs as well. His more important conclusion is this: "Firms with broadly educated leadership are probably no more profitable than others. But they may be more innovative, more risk-taking, and more socially responsive. If so, the impact of a liberal education goes far beyond advantaging some managers and some forms over others. Though indirect in effect, liberal education may be helping to facilitate industrial change, stimulate entrepreneurship, and improve the general quality of work life in America."

B - "Liberal Education and the Corporation," Bernard Murchland, Professor of Philosophy, Ohio Wesleyan University.

D - **Liberal Education and Corporate America**. Center for Applied Social Science, Boston University, 1988.

This reports on a survey of employers and employing organizations and middle and senior level managers concerning their policies and preferences on hiring liberal arts alumni. The results showed that a fourth of the firms recruited liberal arts graduates on the campus and half offer on-the-job training for which liberal arts alumni are eligible. The corporations reported that the areas of greatest opportunity for liberal arts graduates may be in marketing and sales.

S - "Liberal Education: Preparation for Life." Joseph S. Johnston, **Private Colleges**, Carnegie Communications, New York, NY.

S - "Liberal Education and Preparation for Work," Chickering, A.W., **Teaching Excellence for a Learning Society**, Austin, TX, National Institute for Staff and Organizational Development, 1984.

S - "A Liberal Education IS Preparation for Work." Robert G. O'Neal and Wayne E. Wallace. **Journal of College Placement**, Summer , 1980, pp. 61-66.

S - **Liberal Education and the World of Work**. T.P. O'Malley, Cleveland: John Carroll University, 1980.

A most thoughtful statement by the President of John Carroll University regarding the importance of a liberal education. He reports that 80% to 90% of his graduates have careers that are "discontinuous with their majors as undergraduates". "He states well the difficulty of communicating this to liberal arts students: "Unable to imagine themselves 10, 20,or 30 years hence, they suppose, in their late teens and early twenties, that all discoveries have already been made, that their futures are tied by a Gordian Knot to existing industries and professions, that no new technologies and disciplines will develop, and that they can't possibly wind up doing different things from what they start out to do."

S - "Liberal Education? You've Gotta Be Kidding." John L. Munschauer, **FORUM**, Association of American Colleges, November, 1980.

B - **Liberal Learning and Business Careers,** Thomas B. Jones (Ed.), Metropolitan State University, St. Paul Minnesota, May, 1982.

C - **Liberal Learning and Career Preparation.** Mary Ann F. Rehnke, editor. Washington: American Association for Higher Education, 1983.

B - **Liberal Learning and the Corporation**, Thomas H. Wyman, an address given at Dickinson College, November 14, 1985.

The former chief executive officer of CBS says, "I am convinced that the future leadership of Corporate America will depend on those who have experienced the varied rigors of a liberal arts education as opposed to narrower, more specialized courses of instruction." In this address, he referred to CBS' $750,000 grant to form the Corporate Council on the Liberal Arts, for the purpose of examining the influence which a liberal arts education has on effective business leadership. Wyman gives examples of CBS work with liberal arts faculty, in probing for solutions to the problems of their corporation.

MS - "Liberal Learning is a Sound Human Capital Investment." Kathryn Mohrman. **Educational Record**, Fall, 1983.

Mohrman cites studies which indicate that a liberal education yields a greater return on investment than specialized college training, because "in a mobile society, workers are likely to benefit for a longer time from general education and training." She gives numerous examples of corporations (CIGNA, American Can, etc.) and universities/colleges (Rice, Wheaton, Metropolitan State, Gustavus-Adolphus, etc.) which are working together to link liberal learning with understandings of business leadership.

B - "Liberal Learning and the World: A Banker's Perspective," Robert J. Callander, **Liberal Education,** 1986, Volume 72, No. 1.

D - **Life After Liberal Arts—And What to Do During Liberal Arts.** Richard S. Benner and Susan Tyler Hitchcock, Office of Career Planning and Placement, University of Virginia, 1985.

Information and advice for students from the University's 1984 College of Arts & Sciences Alumni Career Survey. The booklet offers considerable evidence of the success and satisfaction of liberal arts graduates, an analysis of the skills and attributes that they can offer an employer, and a four-year plan for liberal arts students seeking to maximize their career potential. The authors also suggest campus activities that can help one's career preparation. Alumni respondents provide detailed advice and cogent quotes regarding the best methods for job-hunting. In all, this is an excellent manual for any graduate seeking confidence and a strong rationale for his or her job marketability.

C - **Life After Shakespeare: Careers for Liberal Arts Majors**. Manuel Flores-Esteves, New York: Penguin Books, 1985.

This 143-page book is a most compact and yet detailed compilation of jobs for liberal arts graduates. It is organized to include numerous job definitions in each of the following categories— advertising, airlines and travel, business management, consulting, consumer protection, cultural organizations, education, environmental protection, finance, foreign affairs, fund-raising, government, insurance, international service, labor unions, lobbying, opinion polls and surveys, personnel, politics, public affairs, publishing, radio-TV, real estate, recreation, research, sales, social services, and writing. As you can see, the author has covered the waterfront exceptionally well. The contents of this book are ample evidence that there is a virtual candy-store of possibilities for non-technical and non-specialized college graduates. The book includes names of professional associations that will provide (free) more information about specific careers, and names of key organizations related to particular fields of work.

S - "Life/Career Planning and the Liberal Arts." Richard S. Benner and David L. Potter, **Liberal Education,** 1981. Volume 67, No. 1, pp. 71-87.

CR - "The Major Decision." Will Kollock, **DORM Magazine**, Spring, 1985

The author, chairperson of communication arts at Ramapo College, explains why engineering graduates make the highest starting salaries (and liberal arts graduates usually make the lowest), yet liberal arts graduates are more likely to reach positions of leadership and have prosperous careers.

B - "Managing our Way to Economic Decline." Robert Hayes and William Abernathy. **Harvard Business Review**, July-August 1980.

The authors explain why they believe modern management principles are short-sighted and have contributed to the decline of the U.S.A.'s productivity, compared to other countries. The article states that an excessive focus on short-term profitability obscures the need for wider vision and imagination. This is relevant to liberal education, as its graduates are often noted for their 'big picture' thinking and imagination. Thus, the liberal arts graduate may have qualities which would help to reverse the trend toward economic decline.

C - "Mind-Stretching Exercises for Liberal Arts Grads." Edward P. Duggan. **Journal of College Placement,** Winter 1982, pp.23-24.

CR - "More Adults Return to College to Study the Liberal Arts ." Beverly T. Watkins. **Chronicle of Higher Education**, April 25, 1985, pp. 1, 12.

CR - **A New Case For the Liberal Arts**. Winter, David, McCelland, David, and Stewart, Abigail. San Francisco, Jossey-Bass, 1981.

The authors report the results of several cross-sectional and longitudinal studies of students at liberal arts colleges and other post-secondary institutions to demonstrate that liberal arts education has beneficial effects not produced by any other kind of training. Using findings from a 14-year study of liberal arts graduates, they show that liberal education contributes significantly to success in later life and that it produces benefits for society as well, through better leadership and management skills, and the more vigorous participation in civic organizations of college graduates. This book takes the lofty goals of liberal education and translates them into measurable effects that can be understood by both college graduates and the employers for whom they hope to work.

S - "New Findings on the Links Between College Education and Work." Lewis C. Solmon. **Higher Education,** 1981, 10 pp. 615-648.

CR - "A New Liberal Arts Curriculum for The Age of Technology." Donald Hockney and George Bugliarello. **The Bent of Tau Beta Pi**, November 1985.

The authors describe a new curriculum designed at the Polytechnic Institute of New York, in which liberal arts students are given numerous courses which examine technological themes, including "Technology and Society in Historical Perspective," "The World of Biology", "Machines - Extensions of Man," and many others. They propose that today's curriculum for any liberal arts student must incorporate technological themes. I agree with their view that the reverse should hold as well—technological curricula must address humanities issues and other liberal arts themes and perspectives. Each of these curricular blends will perhaps be slow in coming, but they are crucial if we are to bridge what C.P. Snow calls the "two cultures" of contemporary life.

B - **New Links Between General Education and Business Careers**, Russell G. Warren. Washington: Association of American Colleges, 1983.

Results from a survey of 113 medium and large-sized businesses revealed the skills, attitudes, and knowledge most important to success (interpersonal skills, reasoning ability, and verbal communication skills topped the list), items most important to success in middle or top management positions (verbal communication skills, ability to identify and formulate problems, and willingness to assume responsibility were the highest), and deficiencies in business employees (writing skills was far ahead of the others).

B - **The Newly Promoted Executive: A Study in Corporate Leadership**. Floyd A. Bond, Herbert W. Hildebrandt, Edwin L. Miller. 1983-84 Univ. of Michigan

C - "Philosophy Majors in Demand." Elizabeth M . Fowler, **New York Times**, March 4, 1986.

The "Careers" columnist for the Times reports that philosophy majors are desired by industry and other employers because of their ability to formulate problems (related to computer programming), their ability to think logically, and their ability to deal with abstract concepts. She points out that many leaders in the field of artificial intelligence have backgrounds in philosophy, and that philosophy students are also usually attracted to mathematics.

J - **Playing Hardball With Soft Skills.** Steven J. Bennett. New York: Batam Books, 1986.

The author is a refugee from an academic PhD. program. He explains how a person with "soft" (non-vocational) skills can prosper as an entrepreneur in a high-tech world. He explains how to inventory your personal strengths, how to sense the opportunities in high-tech, and how to market yourself and your ideas. Much of the book's emphasis is on entrepreneurship, as he outlines how to develop, fund, and market new ideas for products or services.

D - **A Post-Graduate Survey of Liberal Arts Majors 1968, 1973 and 1978**. James M. Slick. Pennsylvania State University, 1981.

B - "Preparing Liberal Arts Students for Careers in Business." Richard J. Ritchie. **Journal of College Placement**, Winter 1983, pp. 53-56.

J - **Public and Nonprofit Sector Employment for Liberal Arts Graduates**. Christopher J. Shinkman, Washington: Association of American Colleges, 1982.

This survey of employers and colleges reveals that public service and nonprofit organizations have a very low participation rate in campus recruitment programs, compared to the participation of profit-making organizations. The author, a leader in the career planning and placement field, presents a strong argument for developing balance in recruitment programs, lest students mistakenly believe that there are few jobs in the nonprofit sector. The booklet includes an excellent bibliography of career resources related to employment in nonprofit organizations.

S - **Putting Liberal Arts to Work**. William A. Cook and James C. Gonyea. New England Center for Career Development, October, 1981.

Job search for liberal arts graduates.

S - "Real Career Education Comes from the Liberal Arts." Edwin J. Delattre. **Teaching Political Science**. Spring, 1983

The author, the President of St. John's College, asserts that students mistake job preparation for a career. The latter is the work one chooses to invest one's life in. It can include one's paid work, family raising, philanthropy, personal or community interests, or some combination of these. The point is that the pursuit of mere income and security demeans the word "career." Doing work that has some effect upon the world is more worthy of the word "career." Delattre believes that students must understand this concept if they are to have any career success at all. He also believes that the liberal education is the only real career preparation. His inference is that a liberal education fosters the larger definition of "career" that he believes is necessary. An excellent discussion of the different meanings of work, job, career, etc. is found in Thomas Green's **Work, Leisure, and the American Schools.** (Random House, New York, 1968).

J - "The Real World and the Liberal Arts Degree— Can You Get There from Here?," Patricia M. Alley. **Journal of College Placement**, Winter 1985.

A survey of Williamette College liberal arts graduates confirmed the results of similar studies at other institutions, in that they are found in a wide variety of jobs and careers. The unique result was that 34% of the respondents stated that their current position was not related to their academic major and that they would like a related job but cannot find one. The graduates view this state as "underemployment," even though longitudinal studies show that one's undergraduate major does not either predict or hinder future career success. As Alley says: "they seem to accept the myth of underemployment as fact."

CR - **To Reclaim a Legacy.** William J. Bennett, Washington National Endowment of the Humanities, 1984.

This is a study of the humanities curricula at American colleges and universities. Its major findings include: "The humanities, and particularly the study of Western civilization, have lost their central place in the undergraduate curriculum...A student can obtain a bachelor's degree from 75% of all American colleges and universities without having studied European history, from 72% without having studied American literature or history...fewer than half of all colleges and universities now require foreign language study." Bennett concludes: "On too many campuses, the curriculum has become a self-service cafeteria through which students pass without being nourished." This report suggests that the "liberal education" we prize may be in some disarray, and that possibly the benefits of such an education in the marketplace may suffer, unless the key curricular themes of a liberal education are restored.

C - "Revenge of the Nerds Backfires." Chris Lee. **Training,** November 1985. page 8.

S - **The Role of the Liberal Arts in Technological Society**, Robert L. Payton. Exxon Education Foundation, September 20, 1983.

S - "Setting Sail Against the Drift." Kathleen Feeley, **The Baltimore Sunday Sun**, September 7, 1980.

CR - "The Shame of Professional Schools." Andrew Hacker, **Harper's**, October

C - **Sociology, Liberal Arts, and Career Preparation**, Dr. Stephen G. Cobb. Orange City, Iowa, Department of Sociology, Northwestern College, 1982.

S - "A Solution to the Liberal Arts Dilemma." Patricia W. Lunneborg. **Journal of Career Planning & Employment**, Winter 1986, pp. 24-26.

This article is based on the author's publication at the University of Washington, called Putting the liberal arts to work: employers advice to UW students (Seattle, Washington, 1985). It offers much advice to liberal arts students seeking employment. In a study of the nine skills most sought by employers of college graduates, Lunneborg found that employers believe liberal arts graduates excel in "interacting effectively," "speaking effectively," and "using tact, diplomacy, and discretion." However, employers believe that business graduates excel in "managing time, energy, and resources," "identifying problems and needs," "expertise in accounting," and "evaluating information against appropriate standards." The booklet also emphasizes the importance of having leadership roles during college, and defines three types of leadership—project completion, coordination, and taking charge.

M - **Steps to Professional Employment—With Special Advice for Liberal Arts Graduates**. J.K. Hillstrom. Woodbury, NY: Barron's Educational Series, Inc., 1982.

J - **Strategies for Relating Career Preparation and Liberal Learning**. R. Eugene Rice. St. Paul, MN: Northwest Area Foundation Report, 1983.

CR - **Strengthening the Ties That Bind: Integrating Undergraduate Liberal and Professional Study.** Professional Preparation Projects, University of Michigan at Ann Arbor, 1988.

The product of a study made by faculty members from liberal arts and professional departments, this report calls for an integration of the two types of learning. It hopes to begin that process by fostering better communications on the campus.

S - "Study Indicates Liberal Arts Provide Transferable Skills." **Spotlight** (College Placement Council) January 1982, p. 1.

B - "Surprise! Liberal Arts Students Make the Best Managers." Peter Hall, **Business Week's Guide to Careers**, Fall/Winter 1983.

"Are Renaissance men and women destined for the tar pits of managerial history?" the author asks. On the contrary, citing the results of the AT&T study (see The Liberal Arts Major in Bell System Management above), he indicates that liberal arts graduates have strong managerial potential. By contrast, AT&T found "the engineers have all those labs and they don't have the opportunity to develop leadership skills." In the final analysis, the individual matters most: "The type of degree you have has less to do with our success than the kind of approach you have to life," says Leo J. Corbett, Salomon (Brothers) vice-president for sales management.

J - "Targeting Emerging Industries." Nicholas Basta. **Business Week's Guide to Careers**, September, 1985.

The author reaffirms the well-known fact that "the most powerful job generators in the U.S. economy are small, new companies." According to Dun and Bradstreet, only 18% of new jobs will come from firms having 1000+ employees, while 53% will come from firms having fewer than 100 workers. This offers a strong message to liberal arts graduates regarding where they might find their entry-level employment. It also reminds them that the greater number of opportunities lie outside the campus recruitment programs, which are dominated by the largest corporations.

CR - "Technology Literacy Urged for Students in the Liberal Arts." Beverly T. Watkins, **Chronicle of Higher Education**, January 13, 1982, pp. 1 & 11.

The author cites the lack of attention given to technology in the traditional liberal arts education. She indicates that the Alfred Sloan Foundation has directed money toward correcting this deficiency. She cites flush toilets as an example of how technology can relate to the human problem of water conservation and waste disposal, indicating that social scientists and government officials have not explored the possibility of a waterless toilet. She points out that many liberal arts faculty are conversant with computers and research techniques, but they often resist applying their knowledge to "practical" problems. For example, she says, a faculty member may write a paper damning "technology" and then get on a plane to attend a conference where he or she will deliver the paper.

J - "The Inflated Degree." Thomas Moore. **Philadelphia Magazine**, January, 1982.

The author questions the "value" of a college degree in economic terms, given the increasing tuition costs. He cites particularly the questionable payoff of a liberal arts degree, since starting salaries were lowest for that group in 1981. He admits that liberal arts graduates are suitable for the business world, but decries their inability to know how to look for a job. Apparently the author believes that the liberal arts graduate's transition from college to the first job creates a deficit in his/her career progress. He further believes that more "practical" studies during college and less liberal learning would be a formula for career success. Liberal arts alumni cited in the article disagree, but this article appeals to readers looking for an immediate return on their "investment" in a college education.

CR - **The Texas List of Unrequired Reading**, Robert D. King and Joseph M. Horn. University of Texas at Austin, College of Liberal Arts, 1986.

An extensive list of classic books that are recommended for freshmen through seniors. One book per month is suggested for this out-of-class reading program. "The topics covered in these volumes are a good sampling of the most important ideas and events responsible for intellectual life and struggle in Western Civilization."

M - "There's an Art to Grads Getting Jobs - A Liberal Art". Gregory W. Pinney, **Minneapolis Star/Tribune**, Sept. 19, 1986.

S - "Three Factors to Success." George O. Klemp. **Relating Work and Education**, ed by D.W. Vermilye, San Francisco: Jossey-Bass, 1977.

The author, director of research at McBer and Co., studied people in a cross-section of careers. He learned that the factors which separated superior performance in an occupation from marginally acceptable performance did NOT include the amount of one's knowledge of a content area. The key factors were: (1) Cognitive skills (including the ability to see thematic consistencies in diverse information, the ability to understand many sides of a controversial issue, and the ability to learn from experience); (2) Interpersonal skills (including accurate empathy, positive regard for others, and the ability to control feelings of anger or hostility); (3) Motivation (setting high standards for oneself, and the desire to accomplish something unique or do something better than it has been done before). If you are looking for a good rationale for the liberal education as preparation for occupational success, this study provides strong support. Though the "three factors of success" are not the sole province of the liberally educated by any means, these qualities are often emphasized by liberal arts graduates when they talk about their career progress and advancement.

J - "The Three Myths of Preprofessionalism." Paul J. Zingg, **Liberal Education** , Volume 69, No.3.
.

The author shatters the prevalent idea that pre-professional education and liberal education are mutually exclusive, and contends that liberal arts deserves at least equal claim to being "pre-professional" in that it provides an education which is suitable preparation for any professional field. He also attacks the conventional idea of a "profession" and insists that any serious kind of work is a "profession," regardless of whether the person has a permanent, paid position or a relevant credential. He also denies the Blessed Trinity Myth, that "the only ones who really count are the pre-med, pre-law, and pre-business types."

S - "Tinker, Tailor, Waitress, Clerk: Is it Worthwhile to Go to College?" Thomas J. Moore. **Washington Post**, Oct. 23, 1984.

MS - **Unfinished Design: The Humanities and Social Sciences in Undergraduate Engineering Education**. Washington: Association of American Colleges, 1988.

The report concludes that "it is not enough that tomorrow's engineers be well trained; they must also be well educated. The effective program will embrace liberal education not as an afterthought but as a vital component of professional study."

D - "Undergraduate Preparation and Early Career Outcomes: A Study of Recent College Graduates." **Journal of Vocational Behavior**, 24 (3), 279-304 (1984).

S - **The Unity of the Practical Arts and The Liberal Arts.** Mark H. Curtis. Association of American Colleges, Washington,1981.

CR - "The Unlettered University." John C. Sawhill. **Harper's**, February, 1979.

Sawhill bemoans students' insistence upon evaluating their college education as a track toward job and career advancement. He says, "Once considered an essential enterprise for the improvement of American society, higher education has become the handmaiden of a successful career planning."

While many have claimed that training college students to fill specialized jobs is the purpose of higher education, Sawhill argues that as a social philosophy this has failed, because it does not work. It widens the gap between the haves and the have-nots and has failed to deal with numerous social ills.

S - "The View of General Motors on Liberal-Arts Graduates." W. P. MacKinnon. **Chronicle of Higher Education.** (Letters to the Editor), July 3, 1985.

S - "Wake up, Corporate America." Tom Jackson. **Business Week's Guide to Careers**, 1984.

A leading consultant to business and industry and author of career-advancement books asserts that a good liberal education is "an essential ingredient in the formation of an effective, productive leader of American business in this post-industrial era." Jackson notes: "Nothing kills sales more than dull products. People lead with their senses. We live to touch, feel, listen, and see. Our fundamental activity is communication. Scholastically, these senses are in the domain of the liberal arts." Jackson makes it clear that ignoring liberal education in the business world is short-sighted. For example, he states that a better grasp of history might have alleviated some of the problems companies are having in adjusting to changes taking place today.

C - **Wanted; Liberal Arts Graduates - The Career Guide To Companies That Hire Smart People.** Marian L. Salzman and Nancy Marx Better. New York, Anchor Press, Doubleday, 1987.

This book provides ample proof that liberal arts graduates are successful across the entire spectrum of the business world and in government and non-profit organizations as well. The authors describe entry paths for many of the best known corporations, and indicate repeatedly that a sound general education, coupled with sufficient motivation, is what organizations are seeking. Each major industry is characterized with sufficient detail and "insider" background that a liberal arts graduate can judge which may best fit his/her skills and motivations.

C - **What Can I do With a Major in...?** Lawrence R. Malnig with Anita Malnig. Ridgefield, NJ, Abbott Press, 1984.

J - "What Can You Do With an English Major?" Peter G. Beidler. **Journal of College Placement**, Summer 1985, pp. 46-48.

A professor of English surveyed 256 of his graduates and found results that surprised him—33% of the grads in "business and industry" careers, and only 29% in either teaching or words-related jobs. The best of this article are the quotes from graduates themselves, including: "The problems in the real world are much more like what you find in Hemingway and Faulkner than what you find in a marketing text."

C - **What Can You Do With A Sociology Degree?** Columbus: Ohio State University, Dept. of Sociology (Poster) , 1982.

B - "Who Gets Promoted?" Alfred W. Swinyard and Floyd A. Bond. **Harvard Business Review**, 1980, September-October, pp. 6-18.

B - **Who is Top Management?** Ruth B. Shaeffer. New York: The Conference Board, 1982.

B - "Why Business Hires Liberal Arts Grads." **Recruiting Trends**, July 1984., p.2

B - "Whom The Apples Fell On." **Fortune**, January 12, 1981.

B- **Why Business Needs the Liberal Arts.** Smith, Roger B. Address to the Commercial Club of Chicago. (Reprinted by the Council for Financial Aid to Education, n.d.), 1980.

Smith, newly named CEO of General Motors, indicates that 9,000 liberal arts alumni work at his corporation, 22% of all the college graduates employed there. He emphasizes that the study of liberal arts sharpens mental processes that enable workers to have "vision," the ability to foresee how the course of events might change and how the company can respond to such changes. A company's competitiveness and often its survival is dependent on such vision, he maintains. Therefore, General Motors remains committed to seeking graduates who think in this "big picture" way. He states that "our goal will remain to bring the brightest and most gifted liberal arts graduates we can find to General Motors."

J - "You Don't Have to be Crazy to Succeed, but it Sure Helps." Tom Peters, **Austin American-Statesman,** February, 1986.

Peters points out the crucial role that risk-taking, dedication and imagination have in organizational leadership. He cites noted management expert Peter Drucker: "Whenever anything is being accomplished, it is being done, I have learned, by a monomaniac with a mission". This suggests that the free spirit, wide-angle thinking encouraged by a liberal education is much needed in the corporate and nonprofit worlds.

Section 12
What Are We trying To Prove Anyway?

"The recruitment of a number of companies with which I deal is changing from MBA's to high achiever liberal arts students. These companies are realizing that their problems may be due to technically qualified managers who see the trees but lack the wisdom imparted by the liberal arts to see the forest."

Vasser College graduate, advertising executive

In his famous "Fireside Chats" President Franklin D. Roosevelt used the techniques of (1) telling people what he was going to tell them, (2) telling them, and (3) telling them what he had told them.

This section is a bit like Roosevelt's approach because there are some points, perhaps cited earlier, which merit final polishing. And there are still some unanswered questions remaining. One set deals with the overall success of liberal arts graduates. How can alumni, classed as "untrained" by many, advance so far in so many different fields of work, especially in an era that emphasizes technology? What enables liberal arts graduates to get hired, survive the rigors of training, and then take on increased responsibility? "Generic learning skills" may account for their coping with initial job demands but how can we explain their advancement?

Three key themes, which may answer the question, emerge from the data studies and first-hand accounts of liberal arts graduates in the world or work: (1) greater flexibility, (2) more extensive range of knowledge, and (3) leadership potential.

(1) Greater Flexibility

Are we asking you to be like the Plastic Man, stretching from one career to another, having no specific form of your own? No, but a significant fact of working life is that conditions change and college graduates are required to take on many different tasks and roles, even within the same organization. Before long, graduates encounter a task or a project that they know absolutely nothing about. Fear not. In the words of a friend and colleague (Kathy Edwards, director of a mental health association): "Before they figure out you don't know what you're doing...you will."

Those who trained in a specialized college major often feel like they have gotten a divorce (from their major) when they are handed a new, unfamiliar job. They may feel they should go back to school to study a new field, but they cannot. The marketing major who is placed in the finance department feels cut adrift from his or her academic moorings. On the other hand, for the liberal arts graduate who never studied that field anyway "it's just one more new area to learn about." Greater flexibility means "Show me the problem, let me study it for a while, talk to people about it, and I will find a way to solve it." Employers appreciate and reward flexibility because their markets change, their personnel and business contacts change, their products and services change, and their shifting competitive position requires new responses, creative thinking, and adaptability to new conditions.

Of course, business graduates and other technical grads can

Of course, business graduates and other technical grads can be flexible too, but it is an article of faith within the liberal arts that learning skills, problem-solving techniques, and ability to see the "big picture" are more important than prior knowledge of a situation. "Flexibility" is a code word for these qualities.

(2) More Extensive Range of Knowledge

The liberal arts graduate has taken a broad enough variety of courses to feel comfortable in a vast range of occupational fields. A little knowledge, rather than being a dangerous thing, is often an open door to an otherwise unfamiliar field. For example: if you majored in French and minored in music, and your job is a technical writer with a fibre optics company, then your one physics course, two English classes, and your one environmental science course are enough to help you figure out what fibre optics is and how your skills can be applied. Or let's say you are a research assistant in a personnel department where tests are administered, statistics are analyzed, and psychological concepts applied in selection. You were a philosophy major and fine arts minor but included in your college program were two psychology courses, a mathematics course that covered elementary statistical concepts, and political science courses that taught you data-gathering and research skills. That's enough to give you confidence you can learn the tasks involved in this job.

Put a liberal arts graduate in an unfamiliar situation, and he or she finds a way to adapt. As an example, let's say you join a company that imports coffee from Brazil, and you are asked to research the competition. You don't speak Portuguese, you hate coffee, and you have never taken a business course. But, the company sends you to Brazil, you study Portuguese, learn to understand their research reports, subscribe to import-export business journals, and learn all you can about the coffee industry. Your anthropology and history courses help you understand the cultural differences in how South Americans approach international trade.

(3) Leadership Potential

No one is quite sure why it happens, but there is plenty of evidence that liberal arts graduates advance in their places of employment to significant levels of responsibility. Many become chief executive officers of corporations. Many others are leaders in less visible ways—as heads of departments, as heads of research teams, as idea-leaders in their professions, as organizers of community projects, as creators of arts programs, as team leaders of bold new products within organizations.

Be patient with yourself; leadership takes a while to develop. You may have neither the opportunities or the inclination to lead during your first several years of work. But, eventually your desire to excel will likely emerge. Liberal arts seems to

"If the position will not reflect glory on me, I will reflect glory on the work."

Philosopher Epaminondas

"Unless an individual is free to obtain the fullest education with which his society can provide him, he is being injured by society."

Poet Wynton Hugh Auden

breed this kind of motivation. According to Winter, McClelland, and Stewart, the "leadership motivation pattern" is encouraged by liberal education and the idea is not a new one:

"Plato argued that the welfare of the state and the happiness of the private citizen could be secured only under the rule of (the liberally educated): 'Until philosophers are kings, or the kings and princes of this world have the spirit and power of philosophy, and political greatness and wisdom meet in one...then only will this our State have a possibility of life and behold the light of day' (in B. Jowett's (ed.) Plato's Republic, V, 473, Oxford U./Press, London, 1888)"[1]

Liberal education helps the individual to see that a job, a product, or a company are only small bits of information in a larger sea of inter-twined knowledge, cultural forces, historical movements, and shifting perspectives. Liberal arts graduates can move naturally toward positions of leadership by pulling together immediate information with broach-ranging insights. They are not afraid to take on responsibility. They feel their education has prepared them for it. When opportunities for leadership occur, they often say: "This is the chance I have been waiting for."

If liberal arts provides an optimum background for career development, these questions are relevant:

(1) Should Every College Student Throw Off the Shackles of Vocationalism and Enroll in Liberal Arts?

The answer has to be "no." Many college students are quite satisfied to take courses linked to a future vocation. They accept, sometimes grudgingly, their required courses in general education, as necessary inconveniences and look forward to the next classes which they believe will prepare them for future jobs. No amount of pressure would likely force them to give up advertising, interior design, nutrition, accounting, journalism, or other programs that constitute what they regard as their "college education." I wouldn't want to try to convince them otherwise. Like good consumers, they are getting what they paid for. I would, however, encourage a vocationally-oriented student not to take general education too lightly. They should consider for a moment that career success will depend not only upon the knowledge they acquire in college (from their "vocational" majors), but also upon their general learning skills. Thus, the foreign language course that teaches how to communicate with unfamiliar people, or the history course that teaches them how to investigate a topic

[1](Winter, McClelland, and Stewart, **A New Case for the Liberal Arts**, page 2)

to write—these and others will help their career advancement also.

(2) Should Employers Hire Only Liberal Arts Graduates?

Again, "no." Employers have a variety of hiring needs, and many are quite happy to take graduates who have acquired technical knowledge about their field during college. It saves them the trouble of providing this knowledge through training programs. Furthermore, many employers become impatient with liberal arts graduates who do not have clear job and career objectives. And they are right to be reluctant to hire a liberal arts student who may be experimenting with a job or perhaps looking for something to do before returning to graduate school in a year or two. However, employers should consider the possible benefits of liberal arts graduates in their hiring program. Though some are unclear about their job goals, many other liberal arts graduates have investigated fields of work and are motivated and interested job candidates. With both motivation and liberal learning on their side, they have characteristics which can grow into leadership traits.

Employers shouldn't just take my word for it. Individual organizations should study this question for themselves. Look at vocational and liberal arts alumni on their payroll and assess the amount of responsibility which each group handles after some years of work experience. Which are the most likely to be strong assets as organization needs and goals change? By studying actual performance, as did many of the firms whose research is reported in Section 11, each employer will learn the most effective mix of college graduates for his or her organization.

(3) Does Liberal Arts do Something Besides Teach a Person to Quote Literature and Give Complicated Answers to Questions?

Yes. But what is that "something" that liberal learning does?[1]

"Liberal learning should, at its best, help individuals to be

(1) effective in communicating (writing, speaking, listening);
(2) capable of researching, critically analyzing, and synthesizing information
(3) ready to draw parallels, recognize change, and plan for new conditions;
(4) adept at generating alternative approaches to problems using analytical techniques;
(5) prepared for productive work and capable of shifting

"We must educate people today for a future in which the choices to be faced cannot be anticipated by even the wisest among us."

President John F. Kennedy

[1] **Liberal Learning and Business Careers**

102

> *"Literature is the greatest of all sources of refined pleasure and one of the great uses of a liberal education is to enable us to enjoy that pleasure."*
>
> *Biologist Thomas Huxley*

(5) prepared for productive work and capable of shifting careers;
(6) able to understand and appreciated other cultures;
(7) willing to set standards of ethical behavior;
(8) competent to learn independently and throughout a lifetime."

These qualities of liberal learning look familiar when you put them beside the qualities that have been identified as most important for leaders of businesses. They include:

- analytical ability and balanced judgement
- a capacity to solve problems and reach decisions in a sound and well-organized manner
- vigor of mind and imagination
- ability to work with and lead others and understanding of human behavior, as well as, social,
- political, and economic forces

While not all liberal arts graduates develop the qualities noted above, and business students may acquire many of these qualities as well, at least we can say that liberal arts colleges provide their graduates with a mix of knowledge, skills, and perspectives which can contribute to the future success of a business or other organization.

(4) Must Liberal Arts Graduates Have an Independent Source of Income When They Graduate?

After hearing the complaints that liberal arts graduates struggle to find their first jobs, you would think they need post baccalaureate study financial aid from parents or the government, if they are to survive. Financial dependence is a fact of life for many college graduates (including some from business, journalism, etc.), but it does not last long. One to four months are the longest periods of unemployment for most graduates once they begin looking for work. Liberal arts graduates may require 2-3 months to land their first job, but they do find employment. If anyone needs an independent source of income, it is the non-graduate, most of whom have a far more difficult job search.

> *"Their ability to succeed is amply demonstrated by the fact that nearly 50 percent of the undergraduate degrees held by the executives on my corporate staff are in the liberal arts, often accompanied by graduate work in some other field."*
>
> *Finance company executive*

(5) Art Liberal Arts Graduates Superior "Hustlers" in the Job Market?

As liberal arts graduates get jobs, despite their lack of the easily identified qualifications of specialized graduates, one might assume they have streets smarts or other superior ability to talk employers into hiring them. Well, they must be doing something right. In some cases, "connections" from family members or others give the liberal arts graduates a boost. However, in most cases, the graduate himself or herself gives the employer a good reason to hire them. They "sell" themselves as individuals rather than pointing to their academic transcripts.

"The wisest mind hath something yet to learn."

Philosopher George Santayana

They say: "I can do this job. I have the learning skill...writing skill...interpersonal skills...to get the job done." In that sense, the liberal arts graduates are good talkers, because they persuade employers to have faith in them, to respect their ability to help the organization.

(6) Does a Liberal Education Develop Mysterious Qualities?

The qualities, as outlined above, are pretty above board. The mystery is that more college students, their parents, and the general public don't know about them. We regard liberal learning as though it develops in a cocoon. Only when its recipients spring forth years later as competent professionals and leaders do we finally realize that their liberal education had anything to do with it.

The ability to ask: "Why are we doing it this way?" and then search for different approaches and suggest several new possibilities, lies at the heart of their success. For some people, however, who believe that career preparation consists only of acquiring technical competence, the effect of liberal learning upon career performance will remain forever a mystery. Nevertheless, liberal skills should be regarded as valuable assets, and available to anyone who wishes to acquire them. For many college students, a strong liberal education is the ultimate key to realizing their full career (and life) potential.

Areas of Work and Job Titles for Liberal Arts Graduates

The following is a list of job titles in which many liberal arts graduates are employed. A graduate of a liberal arts program may apply for these kinds of work without having graduate study of any additional education.

Acting and Dance

choreographer
dancer
stage manager
actor
producer

Advertising

copywriter
account executive trainee
sales promoter
media buyer
researcher

Art

editorial assistant
fund raiser
appraiser
illustrator
cartoonist
photographer
art director
graphic designer
painter
sculptor

Banking

loan representative
branch manager
operations assistant
trust officer

Book Publishing

editorial assistant
copy editor
sales representative

Computer Services

computer analysis and programming
computer sales and service
operations analysis
data processing manager
statistics

Entertainment and Music

professional athlete
actor/impersonator/ventriloquist
musician/conductor
clown
magician
disc jockey
arranger
composer
singer
orchestrator

Fashion

assistant buyer
publicity assistant
store manager
customer relations

Film

- production assistant
- research assistant
- announcer/newscaster
- camera operator
- cinematographer
- director
- editor
- producer
- program director
- set designer/decorator

Government

- legislative assistant
  (federal, state and local)
- research assistant
- foreign service
- cultural affairs officer
- public affairs officer
- program development officer
- customs agent
- program analyst
- compliance officer
- program information officer
- program evaluation officer
- congressional relations officer
- congressional staff member
- legislative researcher
- caseworker
- administrative assistant
- investigator
- legislative analyst
- economic development coordinator

Insurance

- claim examiner
- underwriter
- actuary
- sales representative
- underwriter
- sales manager
- claims manager
- branch manager

Investments

- stock broker
- research analyst
- commodities trader
- securities analyst

Magazine and Newspaper Publishing

- reporter
- photographer
- research assistant
- promotion assistant

Management

- plant manager
- branch manager
- department manager
- contract coordinator/administrator
- purchasing agent
- project management
- program manager
- urban planner/arts planner
- transportation planner
- land planner
- production superintendent
- station manager (television)
- program manager (television)
- traffic manager

Marketing Research

- statistical analyst
- media analyst
- field supervisor
- export manager
- promotion manager
- advertising manager
- circulation manager
- sales manager
- utility sales and service manager
- field representative

Non-Profit
(association, foundations, research organizations)

- research assistant
- technical writer
- public relations
- administrative assistant
- foundation manager
- community organization director
- coordinator, volunteer services
- public housing manager
- sheltered workshop manager
- rehabilitation center manager
- welfare office director
- community planning director, United Way
- chamber of commerce executive
- director, religious education
- program director, scouting
- YWCA/ YMCA
- executive secretary/voluntary association
- union official

Personnel

- employee relations officer
- job analyst
- benefits manager
- affirmative action officer
- compensation manager
- training and education supervisor
- organizational development specialist
- college recruitment specialist
- employment interviewer
- labor relations manager
- retirement officer
- recruiter

Public Relations

- writer
- publicity assistant
- lobbyist
- speech writer
- song plugger
- fund raising/development
- promoter
- customer relations officer
- press relations officer
- public relations officer

Real Estate

- developer
- agent
- broker
- appraiser
- property manager
- property development officer

Retailing

- assistant buyer
- department manager

Sales

- insurance
- travel/auto rental
- franchise business
- admissions, private school/college
- repair services
- fund raiser
- media space/times sales
- account executive, advertising
- cable television
- instruction
- business services/printing
- commodities, industrial goods
- farm and garden
- hotel and restaurant
- paper products
- machinery
- railroad
- equipment
- plastics/rubber
- furnishing/office machines
- petroleum
- hardware
- textiles
- computers/electrical goods

hospital supplies
containers
scientific products
commodities, consumer goods
motor vehicles
apparel/shoes
furnishings/appliances
musical instruments
cosmetics
books
jewelry
sporting goods
photographic supplies
publications
electronic equipment
writing equipment
flowers
food
building consultants
construction sales
business services

Social Service

caseworker
administrative assistant

Television and Radio

production assistant
broadcaster
salesperson
public relations

Travel

agent
promotion worker
assistant manager
tour organizer

Writing

story editor
screenwriter
book editor
newspaper editor
magazine editor
greeting card writer
poet
author
lyricist
playwright
editorial writer
journalist
critic